St. Olaf College
APR 7 1986
Science Library

COMPUTERS IN HOSPITAL PHARMACY MANAGEMENT

Fundamentals and Applications

Joseph A. Cornell
University of Minnesota

AN ASPEN PUBLICATION®
Aspen Systems Corporation
Rockville, Maryland
London
1983

Library of Congress Cataloging in Publication Data

Cornell, Joseph A.
Computers in hospital pharmacy management.

Includes index.
1. Hospital pharmacies—Data processing.
I. Title. [DNLM: 1. Computers. 2. Pharmacy service, Hospital—Organization and administration. WX 179 C814c]
RA975.5.P5C65   1983   362.1'1   82-24381
ISBN: 0-89443-673-2

Publisher: John Marozsan
Editor-in-Chief: Michael Brown
Executive Managing Editor: Margot Raphael
Editorial Services: Scott Ballotin
Printing and Manufacturing: Debbie Collins

Copyright © 1983 by Aspen Systems Corporation

All rights reserved. This book, or parts thereof, may not be reproduced in any form or by any means, electronic or mechanical, including photocopy, recording, or any information storage and retrieval system now known or to be invented, without written permission from the publisher, except in the case of brief quotations embodied in critical articles or reviews. For information, address Aspen Systems Corporation, 1600 Research Boulevard, Rockville, Maryland 20850.

Library of Congress Catalog Card Number: 82-24381
ISBN: 0-89443-673-2

Printed in the United States of America

1 2 3 4 5

To my wife Judy
and to my sons David and Brian

Table of Contents

Preface vii

Chapter 1— How Computers Work: The Binary Number
            System 1
            Logic 3
            Binary and Decimal Mathematics 10
            Hexadecimal and Octal Numbers 15
            Coding Systems 16

Chapter 2— Programming and Language 19
            How Calculators Function 21
            How Computers Function 22
            Programming Style Considerations 38
            Beginners All-Purpose Symbolic Instruction Code
                (BASIC) 46
            More about Language 55

Chapter 3— Computer Components: Input, Output, and Storage
            Devices 67
            Mainframes 70
            Information Storage Devices 71
            Input Devices 75
            Output Devices 78
            Communication Devices 83

Chapter 4— Systems Development: A Cogent Approach 87

Introduction to Systems 89
Proposal To Perform Systems Analysis 90
Team Formation 91
Objectives Identification 92
Operational System Analysis 93
Alternative Systems Analyses 95
System Design 96
System Controls 98
Backup System 99
Human Factors 100
Testing and Implementation 101

Chapter 5— A Hypothetical Pharmacy System 103

Data Structures 106
Algorithms 135

Appendix A—Glossary 149

Appendix B—ASCII and EBCDIC Codes 161

Appendix C—Sample BASIC Program 171

Appendix D—Sample Pascal Program 175

Appendix E—Sample Proposal To Conduct Systems Analysis.......... 181

Appendix F—Systems Analyses Completion Report 193

Appendix G—A Quick Review of Number Systems 199

Index 205

Preface

Computer literacy—the knowledge of how computers work and how to use them—is a topic of considerable discussion in the 1980s. In more and more homes across the United States, children are amazing and, in some cases, intimidating their parents by coming home from school and casually mentioning the topics they are studying in their computer science courses. Those who graduate from high school in 1990 without knowing something about computers will have difficulty getting a job or being accepted into the college or university of their choice.

The basic concepts of computer science are not beyond the understanding of an average person. It is important to recognize this, because today's world is becoming more and more computer-oriented owing to the information explosion. By 1990, information will be the major product of a significant percentage of all jobs held in the United States. Computers are excellent information handlers. Used properly, they can significantly decrease the cost of any operation that involves the processing of information. Unfortunately, used improperly, they can waste significant amounts of time and money.

Yet 90 to 95 percent of hospital pharmacists practicing today know nothing more about the computers that they are using on a daily basis than how to function within the system installed at their workplace. This book was written in response to this need. It originates from lectures given in an experimental class to graduate students at the University of Minnesota College of Pharmacy in 1979. A similar course is now offered to all undergraduate students.

This book was written to take practicing hospital pharmacists from their current level of computer literacy, whatever it may be, to a level of systems knowledge at which they will be significantly better prepared to participate in a systems development effort. After reading this book, they will have been exposed to the detailed structure of a baseline hospital pharmacy computer system. More importantly, they will understand their true function in a system's life cycle, which involves maintaining, upgrading, and improving the system in which they work. Those who choose may take the models provided and manipulate them into a system that serves them and their patients. Alternatively, they may modify an existing system based on the model presented, thus serving patients and health care workers better. Systems that truly serve, rather than being served, were my objective in writing this book.

No assumptions as to any type of previous training on the part of the readers, other than a degree in pharmacy, are made in this book. Pertinent terminology is defined, and a glossary is provided in Appendix A. The discussion begins with a simple description of the mathematics that underlie contemporary digital computers. From there, it moves toward programming concepts. By the end of the section on language, the reader will be able to write simple programs in the BASIC language, using a modern style that helps the beginning student write better programs.

After a discussion of computer input and output devices, the concepts of systems analysis are presented in the framework of a typical systems development cycle. The way in which the systems development cycle is intended to work is explained, and the reports that would be expected to be written in the development of a hypothetical hospital pharmacy system are presented.

The final chapter presents the functional parts of a typical hospital pharmacy system by means of pseudo-Pascal programs and data structure definitions. This chapter provides a solid framework for understanding the internal functioning of a typical pharmacy system. Although the "system" presented is designed as a unit dose hospital pharmacy system with satellite distribution, the primary modifications necessary for its use in other hospital pharmacies are described.

Joseph A. Cornell
March 1983

Chapter 1

How Computers Work: The Binary Number System

1

Commercially available contemporary digital computers use the binary number system. The reason for this becomes obvious when the way in which computers function is examined.

LOGIC

Asynchronous Logic Operations

The digital computer has been aptly called a "logic machine" because it is capable of performing all of the functions of the set of Boolean logic operators. Boolean logic, which is named after George Boole, a nineteenth century English mathematician, has two meanings in the context of this book: (1) when applied to a logic system, it defines the precise meaning of the ambiguous English word *or* by giving its two possible meanings each a different name: OR for the usual meaning of and/or and EOR (exclusive or) for the meaning of one and only one possibility of several; (2) when applied to a variable, Boolean indicates that the variable may have only two meanings, true or false. Boolean logic operators are the unary operator NOT and the three binary operators AND, OR, and EOR. These logical operators can be combined to perform binary mathematical operations that mimic their decimal equivalents.

A truth table shows what the output should be for all possible values of the input. The truth table for the operator NOT, called unary because it has only one input, is shown in Table 1–1. The NOT operator always changes or inverts the value of the input and presents it as an output. Sometimes two NOT operators are combined, resulting in an operator

Table 1-1 Truth Table for Unary Operator NOT

Input	Output
1	0
0	1

Table 1-2 Truth Table for Binary Operator AND

	Input b	
	0	1
Input a		
0	0	0
1	0	1

Table 1-3 Truth Table for Binary Operator OR

	Input b	
	0	1
Input a		
0	0	1
1	1	1

described as NO CHANGE. The NO CHANGE "operator" is really a nonoperator that does not change the value of the input.

The AND operator gives the 1 result only when all of its inputs are also 1. Any number of inputs may be considered by an AND operator, but, for the sake of simplicity, the truth table is usually shown with two, the minimum number necessary. Table 1-2 is the truth table for the AND operator, with two inputs.

The OR operator gives the 1 result if any or all of its inputs are 1. Any number of inputs can be considered. Table 1-3 shows the minimum input truth table for the OR operator.

The EOR operator gives the true, or 1, result if one and only one of its inputs are true. Any number of inputs may be considered, but the minimum is two. Table 1-4 shows a truth table for the EOR operator with two inputs.

Application of Transistors To Create a Logic Machine

Transistors can be used to design electronic circuits that produce the same results as the truth tables. In fact, devices similar to the transistors used in pocket radios are used to build commercially available digital computers. Transistors function as electrically controlled switches. As such, they have three parts: (1) the input path (collector), (2) the output path (emitter), and (3) the control current input (base). The amount of current supplied to the control-base determines whether the transistor-switch allows current to pass from the input-collector to the output-emitter. Computer designers arbitrarily designated the presence of a current in an electronic circuit as a 1 and the absence as a 0, although the opposite definition could just as easily have been used and, occasionally, is.

Figure 1-1 shows how electronic circuits that perform the Boolean logic operations might be designed with transistors. Each circuit produces a correct truth table (Tables 1-1 through 1-4) according to these rules:

1. If a current (1) is present at the control-base and the input-collector of a nonshaded transistor, the current at the output-emitter will be high.
2. Shaded transistors have a control-base that acts in the opposite manner, giving a 0 at the output-emitter when both the input-collector and the control-base have a current applied, but a 1 when the current at the control-base is low and that at the input-collector is high.
3. Current flows from current sources toward the output.

Table 1-4 Truth Table for Binary Operator EOR

	Input b	
Input a	0	1
0	0	1
1	1	0

Figure 1-1 Logic Circuits Using Transistors

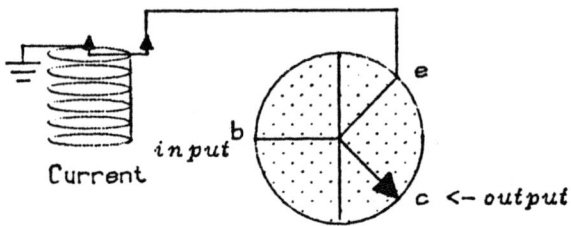

a) Unary Operator NOT

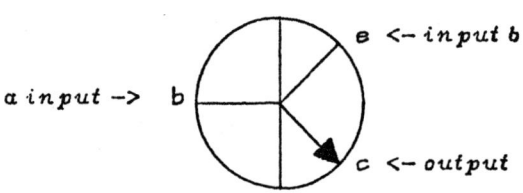

b) Binary Operator AND

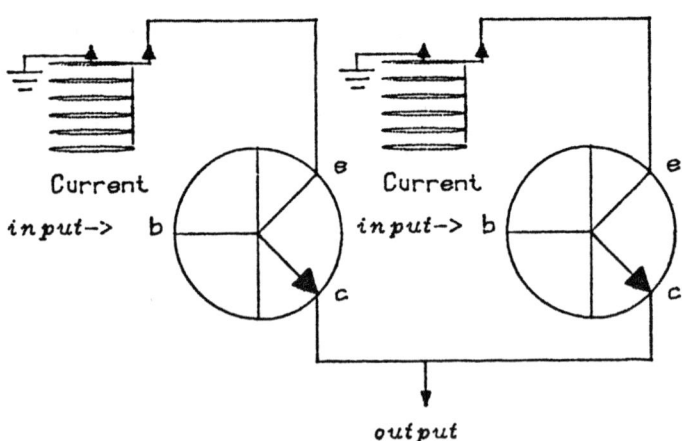

c) Binary Operator OR

Figure 1-1 continued

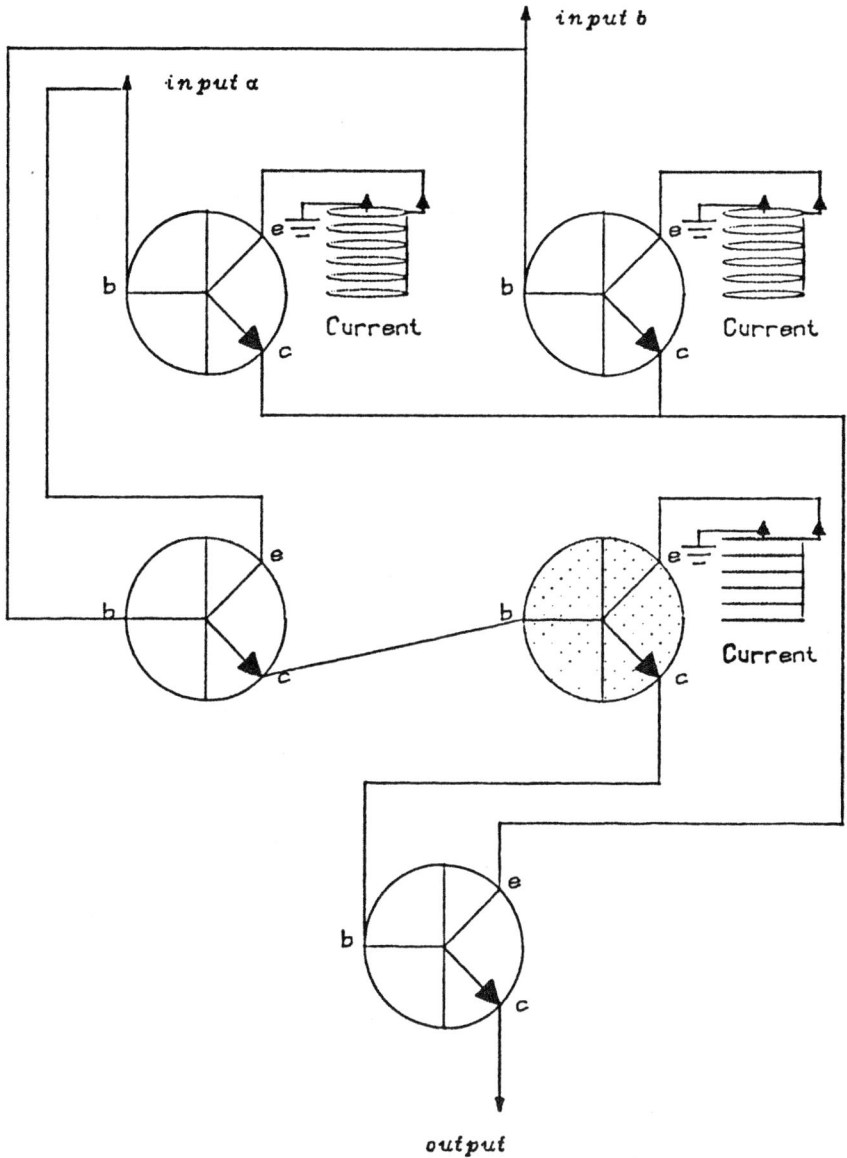

d) Binary Operator EOR

The operator EOR is logically the same as the statement ((OR) AND (NOT AND)). The circuit of Figure 1–1, d, reflects this fact. One OR, two ANDs, and one NOT circuit can be identified in this composite circuit.

The only other type of "logical" circuit commonly used in digital computers is the binary adder. Table 1–5 is the truth table for binary addition. Except for the "carry" output, this table is the same as Table 1–4, the truth table for EOR. The circuit that produces the same output as binary addition (Figure 1–2) is very similar to that for binary operator EOR (Figure 1–1, d).

Virtually all processing of information in modern digital computers could be done with circuits just like these. To be really useful, however, computers must have circuits that can hold onto, shift, and move information. Furthermore, the shifting and moving must be coordinated in order to avoid complete chaos within the computer. This coordination is achieved by means of synchronous circuits that change only when a change signal (clock signal) is given to them. When this signal appears, the outputs change, but they do not change again until another signal is received. The information is effectively stored in the circuit until the next signal. If the outputs of several synchronous circuits are connected to the inputs of others, information can be shifted along a chain, being moved or stored as needed. It is important to note that the individual circuits composing computers are relatively uncomplicated.

Any of the Boolean logic operations can be incorporated into a synchronous circuit if desired, but the unary operator NOT and the unary nonoperator NO CHANGE are the most useful. For all intents and purposes, the other operators are used entirely in the asynchronous mode, i.e., the outputs always reflect the status of the inputs.

Table 1–5 Truth Table for Binary Addition

	Input b	
Input a	0	1
0	0	1
1	1	0*

* Carry output is a 1.

Figure 1-2 Binary Adder

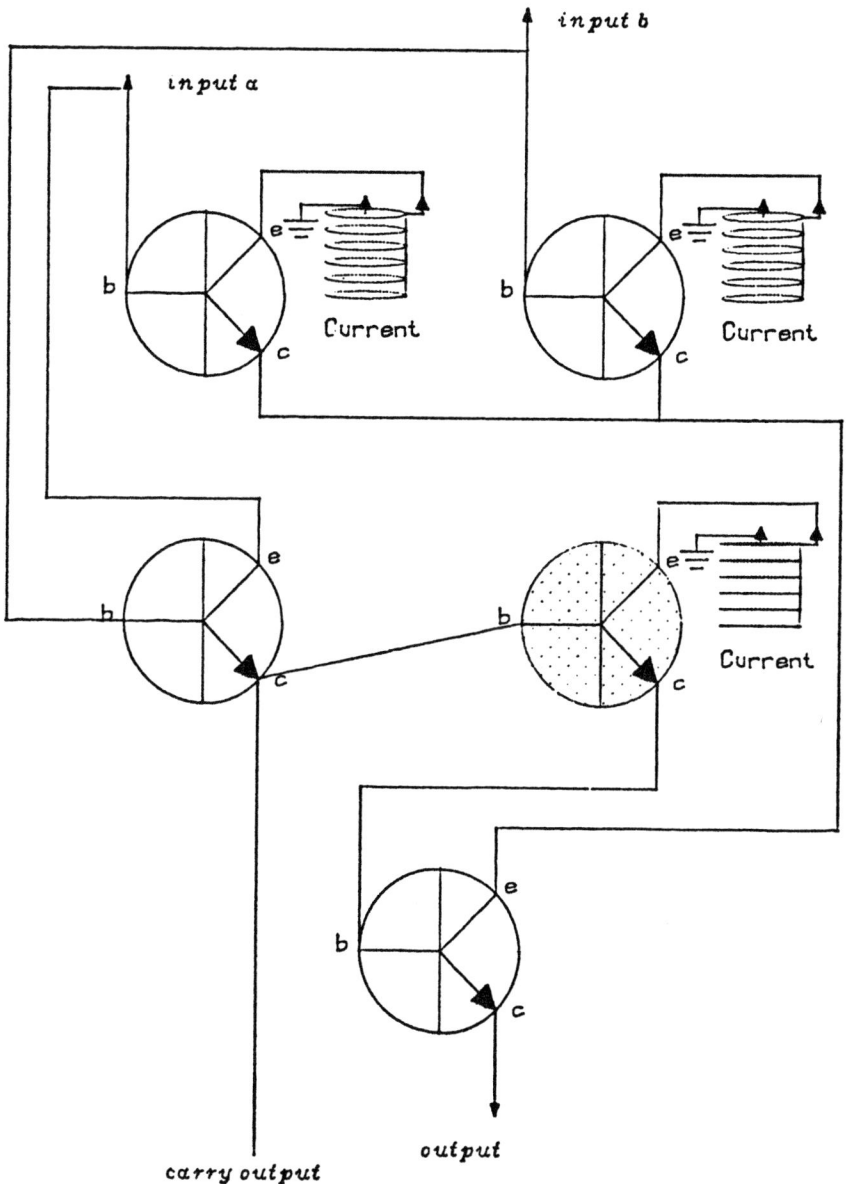

BINARY AND DECIMAL MATHEMATICS

Modern digital computers use binary mathematics internally. The binary number system uses a base 2, whereas the familiar decimal system uses a base 10. (A more complete discussion of number systems is presented in Appendix G.)

Significance of Position

In the binary number system, there are only two numerals, 1 and 0. In the binary number 1101, the rightmost binary digit (bit) is called the least significant digit and is given the value $1 \times (2^0) = 1 \times 1 = 1$. The next bit is in position 1 and is given the value $1 \times (2^1) = 1 \times 2 = 2$. The next bit is in position 2 and is given the value $0 \times (2^2) = 0 \times 4 = 0$. The next bit, in position 3, is the most significant bit, and is given the value $1 \times (2^3) = 1 \times 8 = 8$. The decimal number 345 is, similarly, $3 \times (10^2) + 4 \times (10^1) + 5 \times (10^0)$. The most and least significant digits are 3 and 5, respectively.

Mathematical Operations

In order to understand how computers use the binary number system to perform basic mathematical operations, it can be helpful to compare each procedure with the decimal system in which these operations are already understood.

Addition

Perhaps the easiest operation to perform is addition. Basically, humans add by memorizing the results of each possible single digit combination. If the result of such a combination exceeds the highest value that the position can hold, the part that does not fit is carried. Thus, when 19 is to be added to 28, first 9 and 8 are added, which is remembered to be 17. The 7 is brought down, and the 10 is carried as a 1 in the tens position. The 2 and the 1 in the tens position, plus the carry, are added, which gives 4 in the tens column. The result is then 47.

The procedure in binary is identical. If 1101 and 0111 are to be added in binary, the rightmost 1s are added first, giving the result of 10 binary. The 0 is brought down and the 1 carried. In the next position, the 0 and 1 are added, giving 1, plus the carry, which gives 10 again. Again, the 0 is brought down and the 1 carried. In the next position, the two rightmost 1s are added, giving 10, plus the carry, giving 11. The 1 is brought down and the other carried. In the next position, the 1 and 0 are added, then the carry, giving 10. The 0 is brought down, and, since there are no more numbers to the left of either, the 1 is brought down. The result is 1 0100.

The table of decimal single digit addition products that everyone memorized in elementary school has become automatic. It is often forgotten that there are 51 unique products in base 10 and that it took a significant amount of time to learn them. This table of products, sometimes referred to as a truth table, is quite a bit simpler for the binary system than for the decimal system. There are only 3 unique results in Table 1-5, compared with the 51 of the decimal system.

Subtraction

Decimal subtraction is generally learned in the same way that addition is learned, i.e., by rote memorization of a decimal subtraction truth table. In fact, until they study how computers perform subtraction, most people do not realize that there is another way of doing subtraction. In decimal mathematics, to find the difference A − B, the tens complement of B can be added to A and 1 subtracted from the position to the left by adding 9, the complement of 1, and so on until there is no more space on the left end of the paper; the excess digits can be dropped. The tens complement of a number is the number that, when added to a number, gives 10. The tens complements of all the numbers in the decimal system are

Number:	0	1	2	3	4	5	6	7	8	9
Tens complement:	10	9	8	7	6	5	4	3	2	1

For example, if 8 is to be subtracted from 15, the difference table shows that the answer is 7. The tens complement of 8 is 2. Adding 5 and 2 produces 7. Then 1 is subtracted from the next column, giving the correct result of 7. It is usually an eye-opening experience to practice a few such subtractions.

In the binary number system, subtraction can be performed by adding the twos complement of the subtrahend (the number being subtracted) to the minuend (the number being subtracted from). This would be too difficult for a computer to perform except for a unique property of the binary number system—in the binary number system, the complement of a number is the opposite of the number. It is produced by changing each binary digit (bit) in the number to the other possible digit; thus, 1s are changed to 0s and vice versa. A simple NOT circuit performs this operation. The twos complement of a number is the complement plus 1. Thus, by inverting (performing a NOT operation), incrementing (adding 1 to), and adding the two binary numbers, a computer can perform subtraction. Most computers employ a circuit similar to the adder of Figure 1–2 to perform all subtraction.

Multiplication

Anyone who has ever operated one of those old, hand-cranked adding machines probably knows that numbers can be multiplied by a series of additions and shifts. On those old machines, the multiplicand (number being multiplied) was entered, the repeat lever set, and the crank pulled as many times as the multiplier (the number by which the multiplicand is to be multiplied) indicated. Then the number was shifted by multiplying it by 10, the number entered, and the crank pulled as many times as the next digit of the multiplier indicated. This may seem even more boring than memorizing another table of products. However, computers would not work efficiently with a large truth table. Fortunately, the task is simpler in the binary number system.

To multiply 121 by 125 in decimal by shifts and additions, the first thing to do is add 125 one time, giving 125. The shift gives 1,250, which is added together twice, giving 2,500. Another shift gives 12,500, which is added once. Adding all these results together gives 15,125, which is the same answer a calculator gives.

$$
\begin{array}{rrl}
1\ 2\ 1 & \times\ 125 =& \\
125 \times & 1 =& 125 \\
1250 \times & 2 =& 2{,}500 \\
12500 \times & 1 =& 12{,}500 \\
\hline
& & 15{,}125
\end{array}
$$

To do this same problem in binary, the first step is to find the binary equivalent of 121, which is 111 1001, and the binary equivalent of 125, which is 111 1101. In each position that 111 1001 has a 1, the appropriately shifted value of 111 1101 is added:

$$
\begin{array}{rrl}
1 \times & 111\ 1101 =& 111\ 1101 \\
0 \times & 1111\ 1010 =& 0 \\
0 \times & 1\ 1111\ 0100 =& 0 \\
1 \times & 11\ 1110\ 1000 =& 11\ 1110\ 1000 \\
1 \times & 111\ 1101\ 0000 =& 111\ 1101\ 0000 \\
1 \times & 1111\ 1010\ 0000 =& 1111\ 1010\ 0000 \\
1 \times & 1\ 1111\ 0100\ 0000 =& 1\ 1111\ 0100\ 0000 \\
\hline
& & 11\ 1011\ 0001\ 0101
\end{array}
$$

The binary number 11 1011 0001 0101 is equal to 15,125.*

---

* Unless indicated otherwise, all numbers are in base 10.

Computers multiply in a manner very similar to this. Because most computers do not have built-in multiplying circuits, the user must provide a program that instructs the computer in multiplication.

Division

Although division is not as neat as multiplication or subtraction, it is simple conceptually. Basically, it works the same in binary as it does in decimal. It is much easier, however, to estimate how many times the binary dividend (the number being divided) can be divided by the binary divisor (the number by which the dividend is divided). It is always 1 or 0 (less than or greater than).

In decimal division, if 1,125 (the dividend) is to be divided by 29 (the divisor), the first step is to see if the divisor is greater than the dividend. If so, the result (quotient) would be 0 and the dividend would be the remainder. Since this is not the case, we mask (temporarily cover up) the dividend and then unmask the first digit. Thus, only the first digit of the dividend is considered. The divisor is then compared with the unmasked digit. The divisor digit in this instance, 2, is greater than the dividend digit, 1, so the result is 0. Another digit of the dividend is unmasked, and the divisor is again compared with the unmasked dividend. At this point, the divisor is 29 and the dividend is 11. The divisor is still greater than the dividend, and another 0 goes into the quotient. Another digit in the dividend is unmasked. This time, the dividend is greater than the divisor. Now, the number of times the dividend is greater than the divisor is estimated, and the estimate goes into the third column of the quotient. The estimate is 3 in this example. Next, the estimate is multiplied by the divisor to determine its accuracy. In this case, the result is 87. If the result is greater than the unmasked dividend, the estimate is too high and must be lowered. If the result is less than the unmasked dividend, it is subtracted from the dividend. If the result of this subtraction is greater than the divisor, the estimate is too low and must be increased. Since the result of the subtraction in this example is 25, the 3 can remain. This result then becomes the dividend and, since it is less than the divisor, another digit is unmasked and placed at the end. This gives 255, which is greater than 29. Estimating 8 for the result, multiplying 29 by 8, and subtracting the result from 255 gives 23. The quotient for this division is 38, with a remainder of 23. The only processes used in this example were masking, unmasking, comparison, subtraction, multiplication, and estimation.

As mentioned earlier, the main difference between division in binary and division in decimal is that it is never necessary to estimate how many times the divisor will fit into the dividend. If the dividend is greater, the answer is 1; if it is not, the answer is 0. This can be illustrated by performing the same operation in binary as was performed in decimal. Decimal 29 becomes 1 1101 in binary, and 1,125 becomes 100 0110 0101. The first step is to compare the divisor with the dividend. (This can be done by subtracting them and seeing if the result is negative.) In this example, the dividend is larger, so the operation can proceed. Next, the divisor is compared with the first bit of the dividend. Obviously, the dividend cannot be greater than the divisor until it has at least as many bits, so 0s are entered in the quotient and five bits unmasked in the dividend. In a computer, this would be accomplished by shifting the dividend left from its memory location into an empty one. At this point, the temporary dividend has the value 1 0001, and the divisor is 1 1101. Because the divisor is still greater than the dividend, another bit must be unmasked. This time the dividend is greater. A 1 is entered in the quotient, and the divisor is subtracted from the temporary dividend. The result of this operation, 110, becomes the temporary dividend. This temporary dividend is always less than the divisor (a property of binary algebra). Another bit is unmasked, and the temporary dividend becomes 1100, which is smaller than the divisor. A 0 is entered in the quotient and another bit unmasked. The result is still smaller, so another 0 is placed in the quotient and another digit unmasked. This brings the temporary dividend to 1 1000, still smaller than the divisor, so another bit is unmasked. The temporary dividend is 11 0001. This is greater than the divisor, so a 1 is placed in the quotient. The divisor is subtracted from the temporary dividend, giving 1 0100. Unmasking another bit makes the temporary dividend 10 1000, which is greater than the divisor. A 1 is again placed in the quotient and the divisor subtracted from the temporary dividend. The result is 1011. When another bit is unmasked, the temporary dividend becomes 1 0111. This is still smaller than the divisor, however. As there are no more bits to unmask, the temporary dividend becomes the remainder. The quotient achieved through this procedure, as shown below, is 000 0010 0110. This converts to 38 in decimal. The remainder is 1 0111. This converts to 23 in decimal. These are the same results achieved above.

```
                     000 0010 0110
                    ─────────────────
            1 1101 ) 100 0110 0101
                     11 101
                    ─────────
                     00 1100 01
                        111 01
                       ────────
                        101 000
                         11 101
                        ────────
                         1 0111
```

Most computers do not have a unique circuit to perform division. Therefore, a program must be written so that the computer can perform the operation.

HEXADECIMAL AND OCTAL NUMBERS

The hexadecimal and octal number systems are, respectively, the base 16 and base 8 number systems. The numerals used in the hexadecimal system are, in order of increasing value, 0, 1, 2, 3, 4, 5, 6, 7, 8, 9, A, B, C, D, E, and F. The numerals used in the octal number system are 0, 1, 2, 3, 4, 5, 6, and 7.

Why would anyone want to use a number system that has such strange numerals or one that has fewer numerals than the traditional number system? The answer lies in the fact that people make mistakes when they try to think in binary. Humans seem to be unable to handle long strings of 1s and 0s without making a mistake here and there. To alleviate this problem, the long strings are often broken into smaller ones. If the strings are broken into groups of four, there is a unique hexadecimal symbol for each possible four-bit pattern:

Binary	Hex	Binary	Hex	Binary	Hex	Binary	Hex
0000	0	0100	4	1000	8	1100	C
0001	1	0101	5	1001	9	1101	D
0010	2	0110	6	1010	A	1110	E
0011	3	0111	7	1011	B	1111	F

This shorthand notation saves many errors and allows easy conversion back and forth between binary and hexadecimal. In addition, the 4-bit pattern fits conveniently into the "word size" of most microcomputers, i.e., the number of bits that a computer handles simultaneously. Microcomputers, in general, have word sizes of 8 or 16 bits. Thus, using hexadecimal, two or four characters can be used to replace 8 or 16.

In many microcomputers, the byte is eight bits wide. A byte is any arbitrarily defined number of bits that is given a specific interpretation in a given computer system. For all intents and purposes, a byte consists of eight bits, which constitutes the pattern of an alphabetic or numeric character in the vast majority of computer systems. However, because computer memory sizes are generally specified in terms of bytes and because a byte is not always a standard eight bits wide, it is wise to ask specifically about the byte size before purchasing equipment.

Binary numbers are converted to octal numbers, and vice versa, according to the following:

Binary	Octal
000	0
001	1
010	2
011	3
100	4
101	5
110	6
111	7

The octal number system is more commonly used in larger computers, such as the Control Data Corporation Cyber 70 series. This series of computers has either a 30- or 60-bit word size. Octal code is more convenient for these machines, since five or ten pairs of octal numbers can be used to represent the 30 or 60 bits of the computer word.

CODING SYSTEMS

To be truly useful, a computer must be able to use Arabic numerals and the contemporary alphabet. Unfortunately, computer manufacturers have chosen to provide this capability in a variety of ways.

Binary Coded Decimal

A four-bit code, binary coded decimal (BCD) is used to facilitate binary to decimal conversion when computers are used for mathematical purposes. It is, thus, not really a complete code. It has room only for numbers.

BCD is the same as the hexadecimal system except that A, B, C, D, E, and F are not defined. If the binary pattern for these hexadecimal symbols appears in a BCD data stream, an error has occurred. The usefulness of BCD lies in the fact that BCD numbers can be treated as though they were decimal numbers. A string of BCD numbers can be converted to decimal and each decimal digit placed in the same relative position that its BCD equivalent had:

```
Decimal:   1     2     3     4     5    = 12,345
BCD:     0001  0010  0011  0100  0101   = 00010010001101000101
Binary:  11000001001101                 = 11000001001101
```

Very large BCD numbers can be decoded to decimal using only a four-bit decoding scheme. In addition and subtraction, each BCD "digit" can be added or subtracted in succession, with the decimal carry taken into account.

The binary version of a number is quite different from the BCD version; the binary version takes up much less space. The amount of space required is the primary disadvantage of BCD. BCD uses only half the space required by the two other major coding schemes for storing numbers, however, so it is the coding scheme used in most largely mathematical operations.

Extended Binary Coded Decimal Information Code

BCD is fine if the only information to be processed is in the form of numbers, but other codes are required when alphabetic characters, punctuation marks, and certain control characters used internally in the computer must also be represented. One such code, developed by International Business Machines (IBM), is an extension of BCD; hence, its name is Extended Binary Coded Decimal Information Code (EBCDIC, pronounced eb-see-dik). The meanings that EBCDIC assigns to the various possible patterns of eight bits are presented in Appendix B. The last four bits of the EBCDIC definition of numerals are the same as those of BCD. The fact that there is no simple relationship between the upper case and lower case characters in EBCDIC makes certain data base searching and character manipulation programs more difficult.

EBCDIC is not an officially recognized code, but virtually all IBM equipment uses this code. This makes it difficult to use other manufacturers' equipment with IBM equipment.

American Standard Code for Information Interchange

The only officially recognized standard code for converting binary information into characters, numbers, punctuation, and control characters is the American Standard Code for Information Interchange (ASCII). The ASCII interpretations of the various seven-bit patterns (the most significant bit is not used) are also presented in Appendix B. ASCII is the code implemented by the vast majority of computer manufacturers today.

The ASCII patterns of numbers bear a simple relationship to the numeric value of their binary pattern. By subtracting 48 from the value of the binary pattern, the value of the number is obtained. A lower case character can be changed to upper case simply by changing the bit in the sixth position from a 0 to a 1. When there is an even mix of alphabetic and numeric data, it is common to store everything as the ASCII and to convert numbers to their binary or BCD form for mathematical manipulation.

Chapter 2

Programming and Language

2

It has often been said that the modern calculator is more powerful than most of the first generation of computers. It has even been said that some calculators are computers. Usually, calculators and computers are differentiated primarily by the way in which they are instructed. Calculators are instructed by means of switches; computers, by means of stored programs. ENIAC, commonly considered the forerunner of modern digital computers, would be classified as a calculator by this definition because it had no provision for storing programs.

Computers also differ from calculators in other ways. Computers use the entire alphabet and some punctuation, whereas calculators use numbers and operation symbols. Furthermore, computers operate in a delayed mode. They do not begin using a program until certain procedures have been performed. Calculators operate in an immediate mode, producing the result very shortly after the key has been pressed. In spite of these differences, the electronic principles used to produce such operations as shifts, moves, and additions in computers and calculators are identical.

HOW CALCULATORS FUNCTION

The keys of a calculator function as single push button switches. It may appear that, if a binary machine such as a calculator is to be operated from a single push button switch, it would be necessary to push the button repeatedly to produce the correct binary pattern; however, there are devices, called keyboard encoders, that can convert a pulse coming from one key closure into multiple binary switch pulses.

In order to add 3 and 6 on a calculator, for example, the key marked 3 is pushed first. This closes one switch on the calculator's keyboard, causing the encoder to close switches 1 and 2 (3 = 11_2). The output of the encoder is normally connected via selector 1 to the bases of a group of synchronized transistors that serve as memory storage for the first addend. The next action is to press the key marked +. This is connected to selector 2 opening four switches between the encoder and the first addend memory transistors and closing four switches between the encoder output and a second group of addend memory transistors. Thus, it connects the encoder to a second memory location. It also causes selector 2 to close a switch between the output of the key marked = and a circuit that closes eight switches between the transistors of the two addends and an adding circuit (see Figure 1–2). It thus connects the adding circuit to the = key.

The next step is to press the key marked 6. This closes switch 6 on the left of the encoder, resulting in the closing of switches 2 and 3 and giving the binary output off, on, on, off which represents 6 (6 = 110_2). Since the switches from encoder output to the memory transistors of the second addend are closed, the value 110 is stored in these transistors. The next step is to press the = key. Since the + key has already been pressed, the = key is now connected to a circuit that closes the switches between the memory transistors for both addends and a four-bit adding circuit. Pressing the key causes the adding circuit to add the two addends and store the result (1001_2 = 9) in its result transistors. By means of additional circuitry, this output is indicated on some sort of visual display, usually light-emitting diodes (LEDs) or a liquid crystal display (LCD). Figure 2–1 provides a diagram that can be used to follow this entire procedure.

HOW COMPUTERS FUNCTION

In order to understand how a computer uses a stored program instead of a keyboard, it is helpful to consider first the construction and the operation of a hypothetical microcomputer.

Construction of a Hypothetical Microcomputer

Figure 2–2 shows how the circuits of a microcomputer might be constructed. The central processing unit (CPU) is divided into the microprogramming registers and the arithmetic and logic unit (ALU). The microprogramming section converts the instructions presented to the CPU into switch closures that directly control portions of the ALU. The ALU is composed of circuits that perform arithmetic and Boolean logic operations (e.g., addition and subtraction). The registers are special memory locations that can be directly referenced by instructions. The parts of the CPU are

Figure 2–1 Calculator

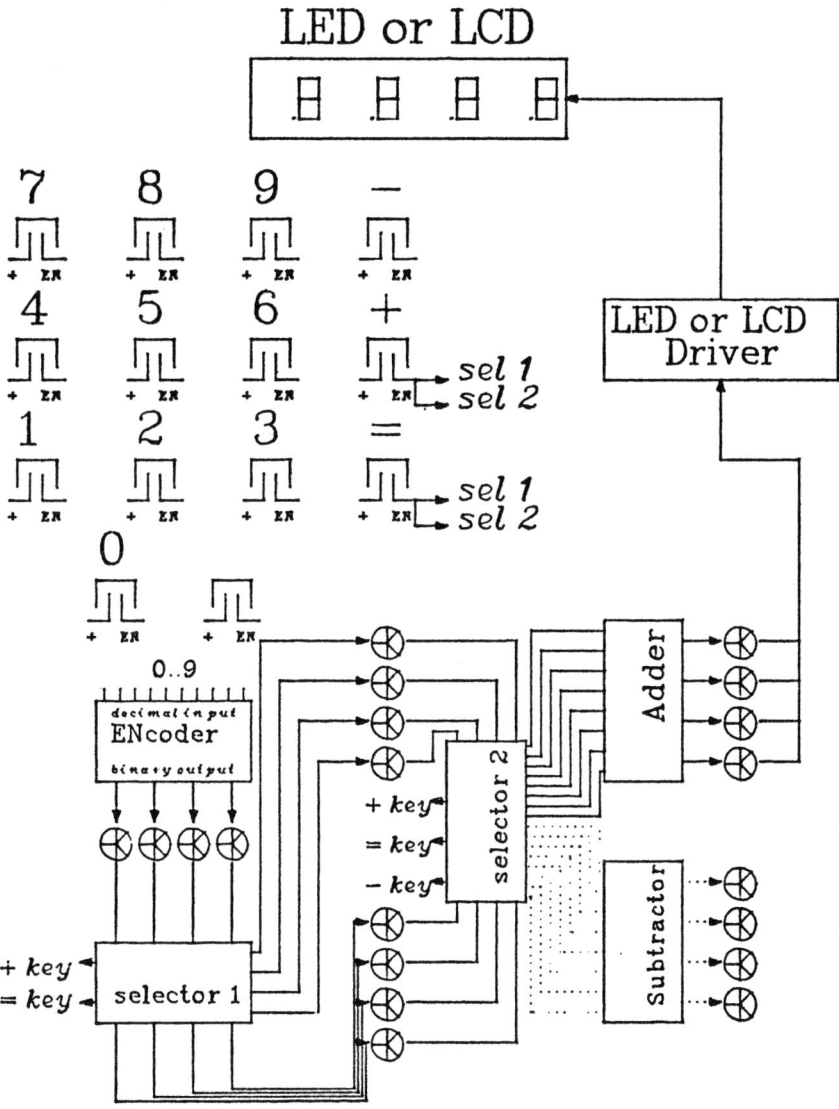

all + are connected to current source

Figure 2–2 Hypothetical Computer: Circuits

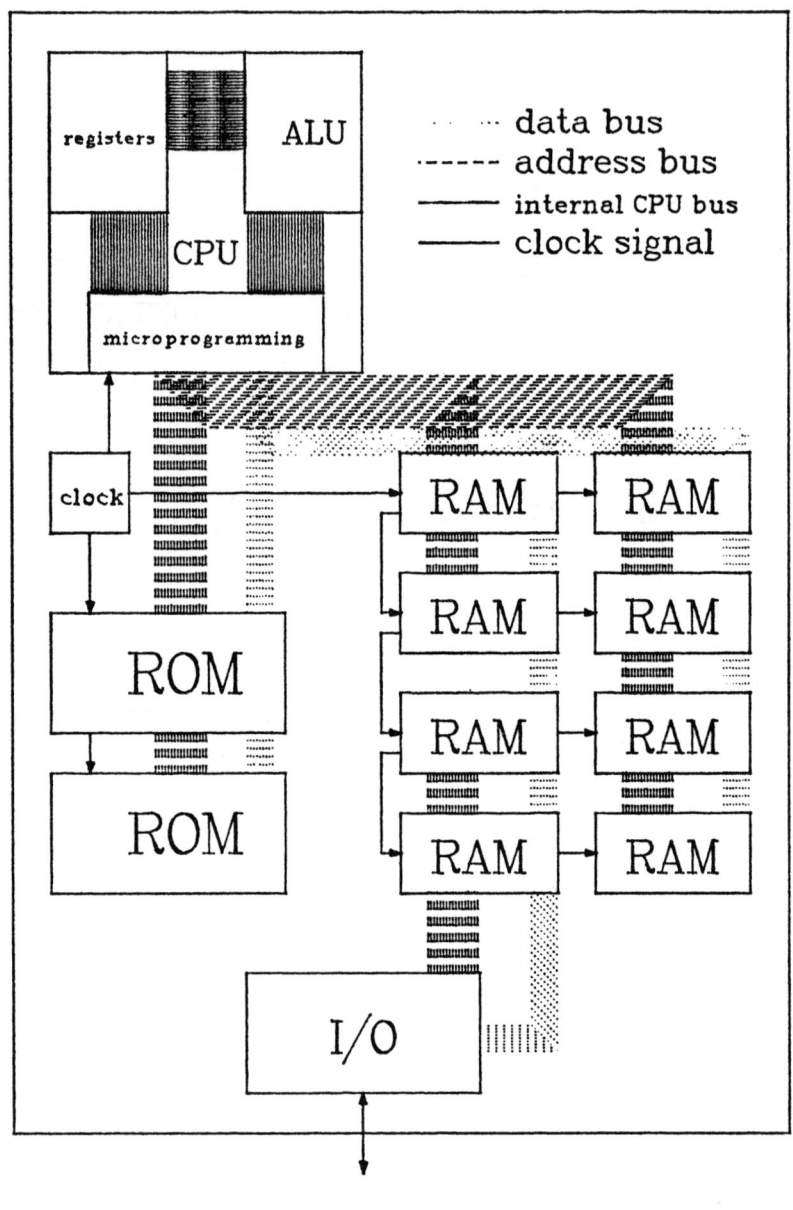

connected by the internal CPU bus, which is similar to a set of parallel wires carrying digital information. The CPU is connected to the remainder of the system by the system bus, which is another set of wires connecting all of the components of the system.

The system clock provides a constant frequency pulse that alternates between 1 and 0. All synchronous parts of the computer perform their operations on this cue, which avoids the confusion that would be caused if one part of the system was acting faster than another.

Memory is divided between random access memory (RAM) and read only memory (ROM). RAM, also referred to as read/write (R/W) memory, functions much like transistors. Since there are typically more than 64,000 bytes in a microcomputer system, however, it is necessary to specify which one is to be involved in an operation. Each set of eight bits (byte) in memory is given a hexadecimal number, referred to as its address. Four hexadecimal digits (16 binary digits) are required to address each byte. To write to RAM, first the address is put onto the address bus, then the data to be stored are put onto the data bus. To retrieve the data from RAM, the address is placed onto the address bus and the data then read. RAM loses its information if power is interrupted or discontinued. (It is volatile.)

As the name implies, users can only read from ROM; they cannot write to it as they can to RAM. ROMs are created in the factory as a memory that permanently stores one, and only one, program. ROM and some other forms of memory do not lose their program information when power is lost. They can be used when the system is first turned on to cause the processor to look at the keyboard to receive instructions. This is referred to as "bootstrapping." Programs that bootstrap may be referred to as "monitors" in some systems.

Programmable ROM (PROM) is a slightly more easily programmed type of nonvolatile ROM. Generally, these can be programmed by services available in any major city. Erasable PROM (EPROM) is a nonvolatile memory that can be both programmed and erased relatively easily. Most microcomputer systems now have available, as an attachment, an EPROM programmer. An EPROM is erased by removing a cover from the circuit and exposing the circuit to ultraviolet light. This erases the entire memory circuit involved. This last characteristic is the major factor that keeps EPROMs from being truly nonvolatile RAM. EPROMs have so dominated the nonvolatile memory market that they are sometimes referred to as PROMs or even ROMs. Those who buy this type of memory for a system must make certain they know what type of nonvolatile memory they are purchasing.

The final element shown in Figure 2–2 is the input/output (I/O) interface. This interface provides signals to control devices that can communicate with people, such as a keyboard for input and a television screen for output.

The logical arrangement of our hypothetical microcomputer system is shown in Figure 2–3. On the left is a diagram of the eight registers in the CPU. On the right is simply a diagrammatic representation of the system memory, which may be either RAM or ROM. All of the registers depicted are 8 bits wide, except register PC, which is 16 bits wide. Registers X, Y, H, and L are general purpose registers used for storing data to be acted on by the CPU. These data can be retrieved either from these registers or from memory directly. Registers X and Y or H and L are sometimes used together for 16-bit words.

The A register is referred to as the accumulator. It is the register in which all operations on data within the system must be performed. The PC register is the program counter, which always points to the memory location of the next instruction to be followed. After each instruction cycle, the PC is incremented by the number of bytes that constituted the instruc-

Figure 2–3 Hypothetical Computer: Logical

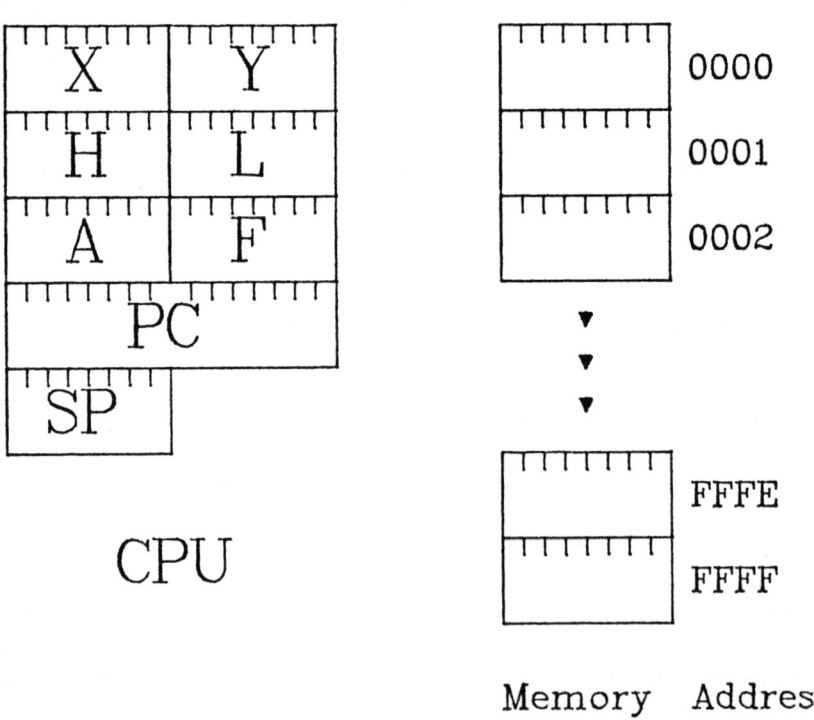

tion (some instructions are several bytes long). When the power to the CPU is turned on, the computer is designed to perform a "power on jump" to a specified memory location, i.e., electronic logic in the system feeds a particular memory location to the PC register. On the following clock cycle, the CPU performs the instruction stored in this location. In this hypothetical system, the power on jump is to memory location Hex FF00, which is where a monitor program in ROM starts.

The F register is a special purpose eight-bit register, usually referred to as the flag or status register. Each bit of the flag register has a specific meaning that can be tested by instructions available in the computer.

The SP register is commonly known as the stack pointer. In this hypothetical microcomputer, it is an eight-bit register that contains the least significant eight bits of the address of the top of the memory area known as the "stack." The stack is a programming device that saves programming time by allowing reuse of program segments. Whenever the program "jumps to a subroutine," the address of the next instruction (current PC contents) is placed in the stack. The SP register is then adjusted so that it points to (contains) the address of the new beginning of the stack. In this hypothetical system, the stack must be within page 0 of memory (hexadecimal locations 0000 through 00FF), since the stack pointer is only eight bits wide. When the subroutine ends, the processor looks at the SP and loads the address indicated back into the PC. The program thus continues from where it was when the subroutine was "called."

Figure 2–4 shows the logical arrangements of several of the more popular eight-bit microprocessors currently available.

Instructions for a Hypothetical Microcomputer

Stored programs function in a computer in very much the same way that switches function in a calculator. With the calculator, the keys directly connect the desired circuits (e.g., adder to memory), and a human provides the instructions by means of keystrokes at appropriate intervals. With a computer, memory provides the instructions, which are decoded by the microprogramming section of the CPU into circuit connections, and a clock provides the timing. The art of programming is to place the instructions into memory in the best sequence.

What are the instructions available and what do they do? The instruction set of this hypothetical microcomputer system has been designed to illustrate the various types of instructions available on many different systems, so it may not represent a realistic set of instructions for a typical microcomputer system. A typical system available today is more likely to have a subset of these available.

Figure 2-4 Popular Microcomputers

A	F
X	Y
PC	
SP	

Motorola 6502

A	B
X	
PC	
SP	
F	

Motorola 6800

A	F
B	C
D	E
H	L
SP	
PC	

8080A

A	F
B	C
D	E
H	L
SP	
PC	
IX	
IY	
IV	R

A'	F'
B'	C'
D'	E'
H'	L'

Z-80

Four types of instruction are typically available on microcomputers: (1) memory, (2) arithmetic/logical, (3) branching, and (4) wait. The instructions for our hypothetical microcomputer are listed in Table 2-1. The leftmost column of this table gives the three-character mnemonic for each instruction. Mnemonics are just arbitrary, abbreviated names given to the instructions by the manufacturer of the device; they have no meaning to the CPU. Assemblers read these mnemonics from a file generated by the programmer and generate an equivalent file of "object codes," which do have absolute meaning to the CPU. The microprogramming section of the CPU decodes each object code into a specific set of switch openings and closures within the CPU (e.g., system bus connected to CPU bus, adder in ALU connected to X and A registers). The object codes are given in hexadecimal in the second column. (Note that some object codes take more than one byte.) Operands, when needed, are indicated in the third column as hexadecimal HHLL for high and low parts of 16-bit hexadecimal numbers, respectively. The fourth column contains a brief description of what each instruction does. The fifth, is an indication of which bits in the flag register are affected by use of the command. The sixth is an indication of how many clock cycles it takes the CPU to perform the instruction.

Memory

Our hypothetical microprocessor allows movement of almost any size block of memory from almost any register (excluding PC) or memory location to almost any other register or memory location. The register-to-register moves (e.g., LXY, LXL, LXA) are simple one-byte, one-cycle instructions that transfer the contents of one internal register to another. The mnemonic, for example, LXY, may be referred to as Load X to Y. With the exception of moves to the A register, these instructions are rarely used in well structured programs.

There are three types of memory-to-register moves. They vary in the way the memory location is specified, called the addressing mode. In the immediate addressing (also known as direct addressing) mode, the address of the memory byte to be placed into the specified register is given by the two bytes immediately following the instruction. In the indexed addressing mode, the address of the memory byte to be moved to a register is determined by adding the one-byte operand following the instruction to the contents of the 16-bit X and Y register pair. The resulting 16-bit number is used as the address of the byte to be moved to the specified register. The final addressing mode in this hypothetical system is called page-directed addressing. Microcomputer memories are commonly visualized as having 256 pages of memory, the starting addresses of which correspond

Table 2–1 Instruction Set of Hypothetical Microcomputer

Mnemonic	Hexa-decimal Object Code	Operand	Action	Flag Bits	Clock Cycles
LAY	01		Move contents of A to Y		1
LYA	02		Move contents of Y to A		1
LXA	03		Move contents of X to A		1
LAX	04		Move contents of A to X		1
LAL	05		Move contents of A to L		1
SLA	06		Store contents of L to A		1
LAH	07		Move contents of A to H		1
LHA	08		Move contents of H to A		1
LYL	09		Move contents of Y to L		1
LLY	0A		Move contents of L to Y		1
LHD	0B	HHLL	Load H directly from memory address HHLL		2
LXD	0C	HHLL	Load X directly from HHLL		2
LLD	0D	HHLL	Load L directly from HHLL		2
LYD	0E	HHLL	Load Y directly from HHLL		2
LAD	0F	HHLL	Load A directly from HHLL		2
LHI	10	XY,LL	Load H indirectly from XY+LL		3
LLI	11	XY,LL	Load L indirectly from XY+LL		3
LAI	12	XY,LL	Load A indirectly from XY+LL		3
LXP	13	LL	Load X paged from 00LL		1
LYP	14	LL	Load Y paged from 00LL		1
LLP	15	LL	Load L paged from 00LL		1
LHP	16	LL	Load H paged from 00LL		1
LAP	17	LL	Load A paged from 00LL		1
SDX	18	HHLL	Store X directly to HHLL		2
SDY	19	HHLL	Store Y directly to HHLL		2
SDL	1A	HHLL	Store L directly to HHLL		2
SDH	1B	HHLL	Store H directly to HHLL		2
SDA	1C	HHLL	Store A directly to HHLL		2
SIH	1D	XY,LL	Store H indirectly from XY+LL		3

Programming and Language 31

Table 2–1 continued

Mnemonic	Hexa-decimal Object Code	Operand	Action	Flag Bits	Clock Cycles
SIL	1E	XY,LL	Store L indirectly from XY+LL		3
SIA	1F	XY,LL	Store A indirectly from XY+LL		3
SXP	20	LL	Store X paged in 00LL		1
SYP	21	LL	Store Y paged in 00LL		1
SLP	22	LL	Store L paged in 00LL		1
SHP	23	LL	Store H paged in 00LL		1
SAP	24	LL	Store A paged in 00LL		1
DMA	25	LLHH, LLHH	Move contents of first address directly to second		5
BMV	26		Block move		
ADX	27		Add X to accumulator	C,O	1
ADY	28		Add Y to accumulator	C,O	1
ADH	29		Add H to accumulator	C,O	1
ADL	2A		Add L to accumulator	C,O	1
AXC	2B		Add X to accumulator with carry	C,O	1
AYC	2C		Add Y to accumulator with carry	C,O	1
AHC	2D		Add H to accumulator with carry	C,O	1
ALC	2E		Add L to accumulator with carry	C,O	1
AXY	2F		Add HL to XY, result in XY	C,O	1
SBX	30		Subtract X from A	T,S,N,Z	1
SBY	31		Subtract Y from A	T,S,N,Z	1
SBH	32		Subtract H from A	T,S,N,Z	1
SBL	33		Subtract L from A	T,S,N,Z	1
RRC	34		Rotate right circular A	O	1
RLC	35		Rotate left circular A	O	1
RRA	36		Rotate right arithmetic A	O	1
RLA	37		Rotate left arithmetic A	O	1
LLC	38		BCD low half A rotate left circular	O	1
LRC	39		BCD low half A rotate right circular	O	1
LLA	3A		BCD low half A rotate left arithmetic	O	1

Table 2–1 continued

Mnemonic	Hexa-decimal Object Code	Operand	Action	Flag Bits	Clock Cycles
LRA	3B		BCD low half A rotate right arithmetic	O	1
HLC	3C		BCD high half A rotate left circular	O	1
HRC	3D		BCD high half A rotate right circular	O	1
HLA	3E		BCD high half A rotate left arithmetic	O	1
HRA	3F		BCD high half A rotate right arithmetic	O	1
DCA	40		Decrement accumulator	Z,T,S,N	1
ICA	41		Increment accumulator	C,O	1
ANX	42		AND X with accumulator	Z	1
ANY	43		AND Y with accumulator	Z	1
ANH	44		AND H with accumulator	Z	1
ANL	45		AND L with accumulator	Z	1
ANA	46		AND A with accumulator	Z	1
ORX	47		OR X with accumulator	Z	1
ORY	48		OR Y with accumulator	Z	1
ORH	49		OR H with accumulator	Z	1
ORL	4A		OR L with accumulator	Z	1
ORA	4B		OR A with accumulator	Z	1
EOX	4C		EOR X with accumulator	Z	1
EOY	4D		EOR Y with accumulator	Z	1
EOH	4E		EOR H with accumulator	Z	1
EOL	4F		EOR L with accumulator	Z	1
EOA	50		EOR A with A (clears A)	Z	1
BRD	51	HHLL	Unconditional branch to HHLL direct		1
BRI	52	XY,LL	Unconditional branch indir to XY+LL		2
BRP	53	LL	Unconditional branch paged to 00LL		1
BZF	54	HHLL	Branch if Z is false (0)		2
BZT	55	HHLL	Branch if Z is true (1)		2
BSF	56	HHLL	Branch if S is false (0)		2
BST	57	HHLL	Branch if S is true (1)		2
BTF	58	HHLL	Branch if T is false (0)		2
BTT	59	HHLL	Branch if T is true (1)		2
BOF	5A	HHLL	Branch if O is false (0)		2
BOT	5B	HHLL	Branch if O is true (1)		2
BCF	5C	HHLL	Branch if C is false (0)		2

Table 2-1 continued

Mnemonic	Hexa-decimal Object Code	Operand	Action	Flag Bits	Clock Cycles
BCT	5D	HHLL	Branch if C is true (1)		2
BNF	5E	HHLL	Branch if N is false (0)		2
BNT	5F	HHLL	Branch if N is true (1)		2
BIF	60	HHLL	Branch if I is false (0)		2
BIT	61	HHLL	Branch if I is true (1)		2
BPF	62	HHLL	Branch if P is false (0)		2
BPT	63	HHLL	Branch if P is true (1)		2
RTN	64		Return from subroutine		1
BSD	65	HHLL	Branch to subroutine direct		2
BSI	66	XY,LL	Branch to subroutine indexed		3
BSP	67	LL	Branch to subroutine paged		2
JSZ	68	HHLL	Jump to subroutine if Z true		3
JSS	69	HHLL	Jump to subroutine if S true		3
JST	6A	HHLL	Jump to subroutine if T true		3
JSO	6B	HHLL	Jump to subroutine if O true		3
JSC	6C	HHLL	Jump to subroutine if C true		3
JSN	6D	HHLL	Jump to subroutine if N true		3
PSH	6E		Increase stack by two		1
PUL	6F		Decrease stack by two		1
NOP	00		No operation, kill time		1
WAI	71		Wait for interrupt		1
CLF	73		Clear all flags		1

Note: In a real microcomputer, these numbers would be out of sequence because of the absolute meaning of each bit to the circuits of the microprogramming section.

---

to the 256 possible combinations of high-order hexadecimal digits. Page 0 would thus be hexadecimal memory locations 0000 to 00FF; page 1, 0100 to 01FF; page 255, FF00 to FFFF. In these instructions, the high-order byte of the address is understood to correspond to a constant page of memory. The low-order byte is specified after the instruction, as in the immediate mode. This system shortens (and therefore speeds up) program operation. In our hypothetical system, page 1 of memory is reserved for storage of data to be addressed later in this mode. All page-directed addressing thus involves page 1. The mnemonics for moving data to the H register using direct, indexed, and page-directed addressing are, respectively, LHD, LHI, and LHP (literally, Load H directly, Load H indexed, and Load H page-directed).

Moves from registers to memory are allowed with the only restriction in this hypothetical system that data cannot be moved to memory from the PC register. As seen in Table 2-1, all of the addressing modes available for memory-to-register moves are also available for register-to-memory moves. The mnemonics for moving data from the H register to memory in direct, indexed, and page-directed addressing are, respectively, SDH, SIH, and SPH. These mnemonics are sometimes read as Store directly from H, Store indexed from H, and Store page-directed from H.

Direct memory-to-memory move instructions are referred to as direct memory access (DMA) instructions. In general, it is not useful to move single bytes of data from one memory location to another. This hypothetical system, therefore, allows only one instruction of this type, an immediate addressing instruction; there are two operands for this instruction. The only other DMA instruction in this system makes it possible to move blocks of memory from one area of memory to another. This is particularly useful in data base management and graphics applications in which the contents of a file in memory must be sorted or reorganized. This memory block move instruction is only one byte long, but it requires several bytes of setup code or instruction. It moves a number of bytes of memory equal to the number in the accumulator from the address starting at the number represented by registers X and Y to the addresses starting at the number represented by registers H and L. Thus, to move 256 bytes from page 20 to page 2, FF is placed in the accumulator, 14 (hexadecimal equivalent of 20) in the X register, 00 in the Y register, 02 in the H register and 00 in the L register. The one-byte block move instruction would then be executed.

Arithmetic/Logical Operations

Mathematical manipulation of data is performed by means of arithmetic/logical instructions. The first subgroup of arithmetic operations is the addition group. Instructions are available for eight-bit additions of each general purpose register (X, Y, H, and L) and the contents of the accumulator (Table 2-1). The results are stored in the accumulator. If there is a carry generated by the operation, both the carry (C) and the overflow (O) bits of the flag register go high (becomes 1 or is set to 1), but these operations do not take into account whether the previous operation generated a carry. The mnemonic for adding H to the accumulator, ADH, would be read Add H to the Accumulator. In other, similar operations, any carry from the previous operation is automatically added in before the addition is performed. The corresponding mnemonic, AHC, is read Add H to accumulator with carry. One final instruction, the 16-bit add instruction completes the addition group. This instruction allows addition of the 16 bits of the X and Y registers to the 16 bits of the H and L registers. The result is stored in the X and Y register pair. The C and O bits of the flag register go high as appropriate, but there is no equivalent 16-bit add with carry.

This hypothetical system can perform subtraction of any general purpose register from the accumulator. The results are stored in the accumulator. If the sign is changed during this operation, the S bit of the flag register goes high. If the resulting sign is positive, the T flag is high; if the resulting sign is negative, the N flag is high; if the result is 0, the Z flag goes high. There is no equivalent to the carry operation in the subtraction instruction set of this system. The mnemonic, SBH, is read Subtract contents of H (from accumulator).

Shift instructions are used in writing programs to perform multiplication and division. Two types of shift operation are allowed. One type circulates the number back into the accumulator, and the other replaces the numbers at the opposite end with 0s. Both types "overflow" the rightmost or leftmost bit into the O bit of the flag register. Therefore, if the right or left bit is a 1, the overflow is a 1 after the operation. If it is a 0, the overflow is a 0. By successive use of these operations, the user can determine whether any single bit in a number is high or not. The mnemonic RRC is read Rotate accumulator right circular. Besides the four 8-bit accumulator shifts, there are eight 4-bit accumulator shifts useful in BCD arithmetic.

The increment and decrement accumulator instructions in this hypothetical system do exactly as their name suggests. They add or subtract 1 from the accumulator. Flag operation is the same as for addition and subtraction.

The logical instructions available make it possible to perform any of the binary Boolean operations (i.e., AND, OR, EOR) on any register, as well as on the accumulator. The results of these operations are placed in the accumulator and, where noted in Table 2–1, flag bits are modified after operation. The flag register itself may be operated on, a feature that is useful in certain types of branching. The accumulator may also logically operate on itself. Performing an EOR of the accumulator with itself always gives the result 00, regardless of the contents of the accumulator. This provides a simple one-byte instruction that clears the accumulator.

Branching

The only instructions that can affect the contents of the program counter are the branching instructions. By appropriate use of these instructions, programmers can save a great deal of time by reusing certain portions of programs, such as multiplication routines and division routines. Without these instructions, the entire program would have to be written in sequence from beginning to end. There are three basic kinds of branching instructions: unconditional, conditional, and stack-oriented.

The unconditional instructions are the simplest. Basically, they place the address of a new next instruction into the program counter. Then, instead of going to the next sequential instruction, the computer "jumps" to the address given by the instruction. Addressing modes are the same as those for memory moves—direct, indexed or page-directed. The mnemonics are self-explanatory.

Conditional branching instructions operate in the same way that unconditional branching instructions operate, except that they first test the condition of a particular flag register bit. Depending on the condition of the particular flag bit, the program either branches or continues with the next sequential instruction. Flag bits can be modified through the use of arithmetic operations or a special Clear all flags instruction (listed at the end of Table 2–1). All but two of the activities that affect the flag register have been discussed. These two activities involve input and output from the system. Briefly, logic external to the CPU checks the parity of words going into or out of the system. If the parity is even, the P bit is low; if it is odd, the P bit is high. The last flag, the I bit, goes high if external logic generates an interrupt. This is useful when the operation of the CPU must be halted because of external conditions. The I bit allows the CPU to determine quickly whether the computer was turned off (I low) or interrupted (I high). As seen in Table 2–1, there are branch on condition instructions that test nearly every bit of the flag register. Addressing is immediate only.

The stack-oriented branching operations are useful when a certain process (e.g., multiplication, division) is to be used several times during a program. They can be conditional or unconditional. When these operations are called, the contents of the PC register are placed in page 0 at the address indicated by register SP (00SS and 00S(SP+1)). Then the address of the subroutine is placed into the PC register. On the following instruction cycle, the program jumps to this address and begins executing the subroutine. When the subroutine is finished, it executes an RTN or return instruction. This causes the CPU to execute a page-directed move using register SP as the address and register PC as the destination. As a result, the program goes back to the instruction that follows the one just executed in the main program.

A subroutine may also call another subroutine. The SP register simply moves another two bytes. Obviously, there is a limit to the number of "nesting" levels that can occur within a given computer system. In our hypothetical system, page 0 has room for 128 two-byte stack addresses. Some older systems have 16-byte stacks. In most applications, eight levels of nesting (16 bytes) are all that are needed.

Two miscellaneous operations decrease or increase the stack by two bytes without affecting the contents of the PC register. These are the pull and push operations. The pull operation decreases the SP register by two in our system; this is sometimes known as a "pop" of the stack. The push operation increases the SP register by two. To "push an address onto the stack" means to put the address at the bottom of the stack, then execute a push. The SP register now points to the "pushed" address, and the CPU will jump to this address the next time an RTN is executed. There are situations in which this significantly speeds up a program.

Wait

The no operation command, NOP, causes the computer to do nothing for one clock cycle. It is used when the CPU needs to wait for a known amount of time, such as the time required to communicate with a slower device. If an interrupt is generated by external logic during the cycle of NOP, the interrupt is ignored until the next clock cycle. The other no operation instruction is the wait (WAI) operation. This operation causes the CPU to keep going in circles until it is interrupted. When an interrupt is generated, the CPU loads the contents of hexadecimal 00FE and 00FF into the PC register.

Combination of Instructions

With the instructions discussed, the system should be able to perform some useful work. Table 2–2 is a simple example of what an assembly language program for this hypothetical computer would look like. The object codes are all that are necessary for the computer to execute the program. The rest of the information is to help humans create and maintain the program.

Table 2-2 Sample Assembly Language Program: BCD Multiplication

Address	Hexa-decimal	Mnemonic	Operands	Comment
1000	73	CLF		Clear all flags
1001	50	EOA		Clear accumulator
1002	03	LXA		Put X in A, low half
1003	3B	LRA		Shift right low half A multiplier
1004	6B 10 17	JSO	1017	If low bit is 1, jump to 1017
1007	04	LAX		Save shifted multiplier in X
1008	15 04	LLP	04*	Get counter from 0004 to L
100A	06	SLA		Move counter to A
100B	40	DCA		Decrement accumulator
100C	05	LAL		Return temporary counter to L
100D	55 10 16	BZT		Branch to end if A 0
1010	02	LYA		Move multiplicand to A
1011	3A	LLA		Left shift low BCD accumulator arithmetic
1012	01	LAY		Return multiplicand to Y
1013	51 10 00	BRD	1000	Repeat the procedure
1016	64	RTN		Return to calling procedure (end)
1017	02	LYA		Move Y to A
1018	29	ADH		Add H to A
1019	07	LAH		Move result back to H
101A	64	RTN		Return to multiply routine
101B	00	NOP		End of program, unused memory

Note: When this program, configured as a subroutine, is called, the BCD digit multiplicand is already in the low half of Y and the BCD multiplier is in the low half of X. Location 0004 also contains 04. The eight-bit binary (not BCD) result is in H when the routine finishes.

* Definition of page directed.

PROGRAMMING STYLE CONSIDERATIONS

The most important consideration in programming a computer is to remember that a computer will do exactly what it is instructed to do; it has no common sense. Therefore, a structured approach should be used to solve problems with a computer. It is also important to remember that it is not usually worthwhile to write a program for a procedure that will be used only a few times. Procedures that are performed over and over are the best candidates for computerization.

Data Structures, Algorithms, and Levels of Abstraction

A program has two essential parts: an algorithm and a data structure. An algorithm is a step-by-step procedure for performing the task at hand. A data structure is a representation of all the information needed to perform the task. Both are needed before a program can be written.

Trying to decide whether to design the algorithm or the data structure first is somewhat akin to trying to decide whether the chicken or the egg came first. The algorithm must take into account the data structure, but the data structure must be in a format compatible with optimal programming techniques. For complex problems, systems analysis helps in the development of both. It is usually best to start a program by creating a data structure that accurately represents the real world situation. The algorithm can then be fitted around the information needed in the data structure. Optimal algorithms may also come to mind as the data structure is developed.

The recommended technique for algorithm development is called modular programming. The basic principle of modular programming is divide and conquer. Very complex problems may be solved by sequentially breaking them into smaller parts. One popular method of breaking down problems makes use of a concept referred to as levels of abstraction. For example, the most general statement of a pharmacy's function is to provide drugs for patients. This would be referred to as the highest level of abstraction. The next level might be providing the right drug to the right patient at the right time. The pharmacy's function might be further broken down into ordering drugs from suppliers, sending prescriptions to the nurses' stations, and taking orders from physicians. After this breakdown process has been completed, the lowest level of abstraction includes detailed descriptions of every action performed in the pharmacy. At approximately the middle range of levels of abstraction, it becomes feasible to separate single tasks for which a program could be written. Identification of this level is a skill learned by systems analysts and programmers.

Monitors, Assemblers, Compilers, and Interpreters

A CPU recognizes only hexadecimal (in reality, binary) object codes, but the documentation that indicates what the program is intended to do and how the program is supposed to do it must be included in some way. This problem has been solved in a number of ways. These solutions are, in reality, all variations of a single idea, which is to write one hexadecimal program that makes it possible to write other programs in an English-like language. Commands within this program allow English language documentation to become part of the program and be stored along with the program in the computer.

Programs (software) that accomplish this may be of several varieties. Monitors, also known as operating systems, are programs that handle input, output, and the manipulation of files. Files are groups of characters that may have any type of organization. A program, for example, is input as a file either from a keyboard or from some other device. The monitor not only selects the input, storage, and output of all devices connected to the system, but also controls which program file is to be operated on by the CPU. It thus can cause a jump from its own memory area to the beginning of another program in memory. The only type of file that the CPU itself can jump to is a binary object code file. Fortunately, there are programs that can convert various types of program files to hexadecimal object code.

Programs called assemblers convert CPU oriented mnemonic files to binary object code on a one-for-one basis. So-called assembly language programming (using an assembler to write an object code program) is considered to be the most flexible and efficient, but also most difficult, manner of programming. Assembler programs usually operate on a file and produce another file that is the object code equivalent of the file. This file, when placed in memory, may be jumped to by use of monitor commands. A wide variety of assemblers are generally available for microcomputers.

Compilers are object code programs converting a language file to an object code program that performs the operations described in the file according to the syntax rules of the English-like language used. Language files follow the syntax rules of a specific language, such as BASIC, FORTRAN, COBOL, and Pascal. Program files generally are American Standard Code for Information Interchange (ASCII) files of numbers, alphabetic characters, and punctuation. The output of a compiler is an object code file that may be jumped to (or "run") by command from the monitor.

Interpreters are similar to compilers in that they act on language files. Unlike compilers, however, interpreters do not create an equivalent object code file all at one time. Instead, they read one or more lines of the language file, create an equivalent object code file, jump to the object code file, run it, and return to the program file to interpret more lines. Because interpreters use less memory than do compilers, many earlier microcomputer systems were supplied with interpreters. On the other hand, compilers generate code that generally works faster than does that generated by interpreters. Because of this, plus the rapidly decreasing costs of memory, compilers are becoming more popular and more often available for microcomputer systems. Compilers for a wide variety of languages are generally available for large computer systems.

Multiprogramming

The most likely way for owners of large computers to regain their investment is multiprogramming. When a system is "multiprogrammed," it switches from the commands of one user to those of another. It does this by constantly returning to a modified monitor program, usually referred to as an operating system, that instructs it to keep switching. If any user gives too many commands, thus monopolizing the CPU, a clock in the system interrupts the CPU and causes it to go to the next user. The program of the first user remains at the point at which it was interrupted until the CPU returns to pick up where it left off. Actually, this usually takes place so fast that each user appears to be the only one using the CPU.

Because multiprogramming slows down the CPU, it is used primarily for large-scale computer systems. Multiprogrammed systems are sometimes called time-sharing systems. On-line and real time systems denote that the system performs all commands at the time they are received, rather than delaying them and doing them in batches at one time. Batch mode programs operate faster (use less real time but the same system time) since the CPU need not be slowed by multiprogramming. A typical large-scale computer system operates in an on-line mode during normal business hours and in batch mode through the night. Users who run programs in batch mode generally pay less; since it is less convenient to use batch mode, there is correspondingly less demand and the number of units of CPU time used is generally less.

Typical Algorithm Blocks

In a modular programming technique, a few parts, called blocks, usually appear in each program. These blocks were necessary in traditional programming largely because modern, structured programming languages, such as Pascal, were unavailable. When older languages (e.g., FORTRAN and BASIC) are used, it is still a good idea to develop and retain a block-oriented style.

The first part of a modular program structure is the documentation block, which provides information that will help in modifying, correcting, and maintaining the program. Since this section usually contains a description of the data structure, especially the meanings of cryptic variable names, it is usually written first. Many modern computer languages, such as Digital Equipment Corporation's version of Pascal allow as many as 31 letters in the naming of variables and other data structures. This has, in many instances, rendered the documentation block unnecessary.

The documentation block contains a key to all of the data elements used in the program, giving their names, types, and meanings. It also should include the purpose of the program, its limitations, a brief description of the way the program works, and the names and functions of all subroutines. It is customary to include the program's author(s), revision number (if the program is modified), and the revision date. Copyright notices usually appear in this block. All this information facilitates correction or modification of a program. The size and quality of this documentation block in purchased programs ultimately affect the value of the programs. Unfortunately, for proprietary reasons, it is uncommon to receive a good quality documentation block with a purchased program. Many companies require a special license contract from a buyer before they will even supply a copy of the program with documentation included. Two factors significantly affect the extent of program documentation that is desirable: the size of memory in the system and the likelihood that the program will be revised or repaired. It is unwise to use the entire memory space on documentation or to spend a great deal of time documenting a short program.

The next block of a typical program is the initialization block. The purpose of this block is to insert data, according to the data structure, into registers and memory locations where they will be needed. This part of the program is generally written after the data structure has been defined, although parts of it are gathered during the writing of the next block, the processing block.

The most variable of any of the standard program blocks is the processing block. This block performs all mathematical and character manipulation required by the algorithm. Most commonly, the process block is subdivided into smaller blocks, each performing a small part of the overall task, such as input, processing, or output. This is how the principle of divide and conquer is implemented. Tasks that must be performed more than once in a program, for example, finding the average of a group of numbers, are written as subroutines. The program then jumps to these subroutines and returns as necessary. Subroutines may be written as a separate block in the program or may be a smaller block of the process block. They are usually all kept in the same area of the program.

The error block is responsible for indicating error conditions that occur while the program is running. It is the programmer's responsibility to include instructions that check on assumptions throughout the program. For example, if the CPU is instructed to read a word from an input device and perform one action if the word is yes and another action if it is no, the programmer must write an instruction that handles the error condition in which neither yes nor no is entered. Usually, the instruction involves generating a specific message that tells the user what the error condition is and how to correct it. Since the same types of errors are likely to occur in many places in the program, errors are usually handled in one place so that error-handling messages and routines can be reused. Handling of errors may be facilitated by the assembler, interpreter, or compiler being used and the structure of the language in which the program is written. For example, Pascal compilers will check all subrange integer numeric variables to be certain that they are within a range defined by the programmer.

The output block of a program is optional. If a significant amount of output results from the program, an output block is recommended. The function of the output block is to organize the products of the program and to display or print the results. Output blocks are also commonly used if an unusual or difficult piece of output equipment is to be used. A plotting device, for example, requires special formatting of the output.

The final block of a typical program is the end block, which terminates the program. Depending on the complexity of the computer system being used, this varies from a simple STOP command in a single user system to a series of commands instructing a multiprogrammed system to disconnect each device used, store certain files in permanent memory, release temporary memory used, and generally return the overall system to its condition before the program was run. Much of this may be done automatically by certain computer systems when a single command, such as END, is given.

Data Structures

Data are elemental descriptions of things or people, usually reduced to numbers. Data about a car might include tire size, purchase price, and number of cylinders in the engine. Data about people might include hat size, belt size, height, and weight. Because data by themselves (e.g., 9, 11, 1.53, 6.023 $\times$ 10^{23}) are generally meaningless, they are given labels and units.

Data elements that have the same value at all times are called constants. Examples of constants are the geometric function π (π = 3.14), a person's birthdate, and a pharmacy's Drug Enforcement Administration (DEA) registration number. For ease of programming, most assemblers, compilers, and interpreters allow the assignment of a mnemonic code of the programmer's choosing to a constant. These mnemonic labels should be identified in a tabular format in the documentation block, unless their meaning is clear. The primary function of the initialization block is to assign these mnemonics to the associated numeric values.

As the name implies, the values of variables can vary at different points within a program. Variables are used as running totals or intermediary and final results within programs. Examples of variables are a person's age and the total number of items of controlled substances in stock in a particular pharmacy. Three basic types of variables are used in computer systems today.

1. Integers are variables that can have only whole number values. These are most useful when the data in question (e.g., number of vials of penicillin on the shelf) cannot have a fractional value. They do not work well when multiplication or division of the quantity is necessary.
2. Real variables can assume fractional quantities. They must always have a decimal point. The number of digits allowed in a real variable differs from system to system. Typical microcomputers allow 8 to 12 digits (exclusive of leading or trailing 0s); larger systems allow as many as 30 digits at the option of the programmer.
3. String variables can contain alphabetic, numeric, or punctuation information. For example, a patient's name in a medical record program would be a string variable. Most systems do not allow mathematical manipulation of data in string variables, although many systems allow rapid determination of equality or inequality of strings.

Like the mnemonics assigned to constants, those assigned to variables should be defined in the documentation block. A tabular format with separate sections for each type of variable is preferred. Some systems automatically set all variables to zero at the beginning of a program. Even if this is the case, it may be wise to set all variables to the desired beginning value in the initialization block.

Arrays are similar to variables in that mnemonics are assigned to data. They differ, however, in that many data are given the same mnemonic, with the numeric order distinguishing among data. Arrays can be integer, real, or string, but not usually a mixture of these. An array is typically used for such purposes as maintaining a list of the names of pharmacists in charge on a given day of the month. This array might be given the mnemonic PIC. The name of the pharmacist in charge on day 3 of a month would be found by printing out PIC (3). The equivalent data for day 10 would be PIC (10); for day 30, PIC (30). The advantage of arrays is that a large number of similar data can be accounted for with a single number. In many systems, this number may even be expressed as a mathematical relationship between other variables or constants. For example, if an array, SAL, contains the salaries of a group of employees in numeric order and there are N elements in the array, the median income can be obtaining a listing of SAL (N * .5). In evaluating this expression, the computer first calculates the value of N * .5 and then looks up the data element of array SAL in the position indicated by the integer value (whole number value) of the result.

Matrixes are arrays of arrays. In general, rules of usage that apply to arrays also apply to matrixes. A matrix might be used, for example, to keep track of the pharmacist in charge of each satellite of a hospital on each day of a month. If this matrix were called PIC, the pharmacist in charge on day 3 in Satellite Two would be determined by listing PIC (3,2) or PIC (2,3), depending on the definition of the matrix. Similarly, the pharmacist in charge on day 20 in Satellite Four would be either PIC (20,4) or PIC (4,20). This example illustrates one reason that arrays and matrixes must be documented in the documentation block. Furthermore, matrixes may have more than two dimensions. For example, a matrix could include the name of the pharmacist in charge by date, satellite, and month, or even by date, satellite, month, and year. The number of possible dimensions of a matrix is determined by the system design and ultimately by the amount of memory space available. In most systems, memory space for each array and matrix must be reserved by specific statements; this is best done in the initialization block.

Records are very similar to arrays in that they provide information about a given item based on its numeric order in a file. An individual's checking account number is the record number of that individual's file in a bank's computer, for example. Records differ from arrays in that more than one datum is kept in each numbered position. Records are usually divided into many fields, with each field containing one datum. A patient's medical record might have one field containing the name, another containing the street number and street name, another containing the city, another containing prior medication names, and so on. An example of a record structure is:

```
Person =              record
First name:           string;
Last name:            string;
Middle initial:       char
end; (record)
```

Usually, each field contains a fixed number of characters. This type of record is referred to as a fixed length record. Variable length records are sometimes used, however. To access information in a record, the record name and field name are referenced separated by a period. For example, write (person.first name) is the actual syntax to output a name from a record.

Files consist of a number of records, but only one identifier is needed to locate a given record. Files are strictly sequential structures. To get to the tenth record on a file, the first through ninth record must be either read in or skipped over. Then the tenth record is read into memory and the record field is accessed as with all records. The following example would print the first name of the tenth person on a file of persons called "database."

```
database = file of person;
begin
For i: = 1 to 9 do read (database, person);
read (database, person);
writeln (person.first name);
end.
```

A program can be referred to as a file of alphanumeric characters because the assembler, interpreter, or compiler treats each line of the program like a record with variable length fields. It then breaks up or "parses" each record into words that it recognizes and for which it can create object code. When all of the code has been written, it is usually placed in a "file" consisting of a single record. Punctuation is used in a somewhat standard manner to indicate end of line, end of record, and end of file.

File and record structures should be identified in the documentation block. Most compilers, interpreters, and assemblers do not allow direct definition and naming of fields per se, although there are some exceptions. Files and records are generally more useful in business applications, whereas arrays and matrixes are more useful in mathematical and scientific operations.

Simple sets are used to indicate whether something is part of a certain group. In a drug interaction screening program, for example, it is useful to know whether cephalothin is one of the cephalosporins. If a set that contains the names of all the cephalosporins has been created, it can be determined whether cephalothin is a cephalosporin by comparison with all the names in this set. Sets should be identified in the documentation block as well. Very few languages (assemblers, compilers, or interpreters) have special facilities for creation of sets, but sets can be placed in arrays when necessary.

BEGINNERS ALL-PURPOSE SYMBOLIC INSTRUCTION CODE (BASIC)

All the command types available in BASIC have been discussed, and an example of a BASIC program is presented in Appendix C. One item is common to all BASIC statements: the line number. All BASIC commands must begin with a number. Unless specifically instructed to do otherwise, the computer executes BASIC statements in numeric order, beginning with the lowest numbered statement. It is usually wise to leave several numbers unused between sequential BASIC statements so that new statements can be added easily if an error is discovered or the program is to be modified. Blocks are usually begun on statements with numbers that are multiples of 1,000.

Command Syntax

As noted, the documentation block consists primarily of statements that contain information about a program but in no way affect the flow of information through the program. The REM (short for remember) command is designed for such statements. The computer takes no action on characters that occur on a line after the three characters REM in succession. This is important to remember because even valid commands given on the same line will be ignored by the computer. Obviously, no variable should be given a name that starts with these three characters. Variables in BASIC may have any other name except for the names of commands.

Initialization involves the assignment of the required initial value to the data structure and the reservation of its memory space. Two commands that allow these operations in BASIC are LET and DIMension. LET has two operands and one operator. The first operand is the name of a constant or variable. The second operand is a value, a string, another constant or variable, or a mathematical expression. The operator is the = (equals sign). The effect of the LET command is to give the operand on the left of the operator the same value as the evaluated expression on the right. If the operand on the left is a string variable, the operand on the right may be a string of characters enclosed in quotation marks or another string variable. Most BASIC compilers denote string variable names by means of a suffix. In our discussions and examples, the $ (dollar sign) will be used as a suffix to denote string variable names. The following statements are examples of valid and invalid assignment statements:

Command	Comment
100 Let PIC$ = "Smith, J.R."	Valid. Gives value (Smith, J.R.) to string variable PIC$.
110 Let A = 0	Valid. Sets A equal to 0.
120 Let B = 1010	Valid. Sets B equal to 1010.
130 Let C = B	Valid. Sets C equal to B.

	Command	Comment
140	Let D = B + A	Valid. Sets D equal to the sum of B and A (1010).
150	Let PIC$ = 0	Invalid. The operands on either side of operator must be of the same type.
160	Let A = PIC$	Invalid. Operands are not of same type.
170	Let A + B = C	Invalid. Only one variable is allowed on left of operator.
180	Let PIC$ (A,B) = "Jones, S.J."	Valid. Gives one element of a string matrix a value.

A DIMension command is used in the initialization block to reserve memory space for arrays and matrixes. It must precede assignment commands if values are to be assigned to elements of a matrix so that memory will be available to hold the value(s) given. The syntax or format of the command has the form of the three characters DIM followed by a variable name; left parenthesis; a number, or an integer numeric variable or a mathematical expression that is equal to an integer or an integer constant; a comma; and, for as many times as there are additional dimensions in the matrix, another number, variable, constant, or expression; and all of this followed by a right parenthesis. The effect of the command is to reserve space for a number of values equal to all of the dimensions multiplied together. If variables are used in the command, they must have been given a value beforehand. Examples of valid and invalid DIMension commands are

	Command	Comment
200	DIM A(3,4)	Valid. Gives 12 memory locations to the matrix.
210	DIM PIC$ (10)	Valid. Gives 10 memory locations to the array.
220	DIM B(20,20,20)	Valid. Gives 8,000 memory locations to matrix.
230	DIM C(A(1,2),8)	Valid if A(1,2) has been defined and is an integer. Gives 8 × A(1,2) memory locations.
240	DIM D$(PIC$,10)	Invalid. PIC$ is not an integer.
250	DIM E((A+B),C)	Valid if A, B, and C have been previously defined.
260	DIM F(100,100,100)	Valid only if the system has a large amount of memory, since it reserves 1 million spaces, each roughly eight bytes.

The INPUT command may be used in the initialization block or input block, depending on the way the program is organized. At this command, the computer gathers information. The INPUT command instructs the computer to print a question mark and then read everything typed on the keyboard until a carriage return (RETURN or RTN) is encountered. This command effectively stops the program until a human being or a designated external device enters information. The format of the command is the five-character word INPUT followed by the name of a variable. The computer gives the value of the input to the variable identified. If the variable is integer or real, the input must be all numbers or numbers and a period. If the variable is a string, any data may be entered (except a comma), but numbers will be treated as alphabetic characters. Examples of valid INPUT commands are

Command	Comment
300 INPUT A "1.23" entered	Valid. Sets equal to 1.23.
310 INPUT B$ "J. Jones" entered	Valid. Sets B$ = "J. Jones".
320 INPUT A "J. Jones" entered	Valid. Causes an error, however, because wrong data type entered.
330 INPUT B$ "1.23" entered	Valid. Does not generate error message unless program tries to manipulate B$(= "1.23") mathematically.

The READ, RESTORE, and DATA commands are generally used in the input block, if there is one. Otherwise, they are used in the initialization block. The READ command looks at the current DATA statement and gives the value of the next element to the variable named in the READ command. After each READ command, the BASIC compiler sets the data pointer to the next data element in the DATA command list. The next READ accesses the next data element and moves the pointer; this process continues until all data have been read. DATA commands are indexed from the beginning of the program to the end and are treated as a single set of data. The proximity of the READ command to a particular DATA command in no way affects whether it is used in the READ command. Only the position of the data pointer determines the value given to the variable in the READ command. It is common practice to keep track of the position of this pointer by using a given variable to count each time a READ command is performed. The RESTORE command sets the pointer back to the first data element.

The format of the READ command is the four-character READ, followed by a valid variable name. The format of the DATA command is the four-character word DATA, followed by a data value that may be an integer, a real variable, or a string variable but must correspond to the type of variable in the associated READ statement. String elements must be enclosed in quotation marks. More than one data element may be included in a DATA command if they are separated by commas. The RESTORE command has no operands, so the format is simply the word RESTORE. Examples of the use of READ, DATA, and RESTORE commands are given in the following:

Command	Comment
400 DATA 1.23,1010, "SMITH", "TOM"	Valid. Note that a comma is not acceptable within a DATA string.
410 READ A	Valid.
420 READ PIC$	Invalid. Data points to wrong type of information.
430 READ B	Invalid. Wrong type of information.
440 READ B$	Valid.
450 RESTORE	Valid.
460 READ B	Valid. What does B equal? (Answer B = 1.23.)
470 READ A	Valid. What does A equal? (Answer A = 1010.)

In the previous discussion of the LET command, it was mentioned that the operand to the right of the operator could be a mathematical expression. The use of LET with mathematical expressions is more common in the process block than in the initialization block. Mathematical expressions in BASIC are composed of numbers, constants or variables, operators, and parentheses. The basic format of a mathematical expression is a number, constant, or variable, followed by an operator and another number, constant, or variable.

A mathematical expression may take the place of any number, constant, or variable, however. This makes the situation very complicated. For example, the value of 2.718 (E) raised to the power of -1 times the elimination rate constant (K) times the number of hours since a drug was administered to the patient (T), can be found as follows:

```
400    LET R = -1 * K
410    LET S = R * T
420    LET U = S ** E
```

In this short program, both multiplication (*) and exponentiation (**) operators have been used. This operation required three lines and at least 36 characters. It would be much simpler to write one line that included all the mathematical expressions, but how would the computer know that it should multiply by K and T before raising E to the power of the result? The answer is in the rules of precedence that are part of the BASIC language.

The rules of precedence indicate which operation is performed first if multiple operators occur in the same command. The standard mathematical operators of the BASIC language and their precedence are, in order of decreasing precedence

1. ** or ^ (exponentiation)
2. * and / (multiplication and division)
3. + and − (addition and subtraction)

Because trying to remember these rules may lead to confusion, it is usually easier to make the order of operation explicitly clear to both human and computer by the use of parentheses. A statement equivalent to the previous three-line operation could be written as

$$400 \quad \text{LET U} = \text{E} ** (-1 * \text{K} * \text{T})$$

Examples of valid and invalid LET commands are

Command	Comment
450 LET A = B + C	Valid.
460 LET A = B + C * D	Valid, but the user may not get the expected result.
470 LET E = ((F + G) * H + 1	Invalid. There are not enough right parentheses. It is a good practice to count right and left parentheses in a given statement to be certain that there are equal numbers.
480 LET J * K = L/M	Invalid. There can be no mathematical operators to the left of the equals operator.
490 LET 293 = R	Invalid. The operand to the left of the equals operator must be a variable or a constant.

The BASIC equivalent of the unconditional branch instruction is the GOTO instruction. The format of the GOTO command is the four-character word GOTO followed by a valid line number of the current program. This command causes the program to respond to the commands at the referenced line number rather than those of the next sequential line of the program. It should be possible to write any BASIC program without the use of a single GOTO command. Use of this command indicates poor planning of the algorithm for the program.

The GOSUB and RETURN commands are the BASIC equivalent of assembly language jump to subroutine and return commands. Like their assembly language counterparts, these commands save programming time and memory space by making it possible to reuse segments of the program (subroutines). The GOSUB command transfers control of the program to the referenced line number. When the RETURN command appears in the subroutine, control of the program returns to the line number immediately following the line on which the GOSUB command appeared. The format of the GOSUB command is simply GOSUB followed by a valid line number in the current program. The format of the RETURN command is simply the word RETURN.

The IF-THEN command sequence is the BASIC equivalent of the branch on condition command of assembly language, with a few added features. This command is used when the function that the program is to perform depends on the information currently available in the program. The format of the IF-THEN command is the word IF followed by a variable name; a relational operator; a number, constant, variable, or mathematical expression; the word THEN; and a valid line number of the current program or any other valid BASIC command. The relational operators are = (equals), < (less than), > (greater than), <= (less than or equals), and >= (greater than or equals). In some systems, GT (greater than), LT (less than), GTE (greater than or equals), and LTE (less than or equals) are the operators used. The IF-THEN command sequence transfers control of the program to the referenced line number if the condition specified is satisfied. If a valid BASIC command follows THEN, the command is performed and the program continues with the next line number. If the specified condition is not satisfied, the program does not perform the action but continues with the next line number. Some examples of valid and invalid IF-THEN commands are:

	Command	Comment
500	IF A = B THEN 400	Valid. Sends program to line 400 if A = B.
510	IF B = C THEN GOTO 400	Valid. Just an alternative but wordy version of 500.
520	IF C = D THEN GOSUB 400	Valid. After RETURN, program goes to 530.
530	IF D <= E THEN LET D = E	Valid. Fails to make sense, however, because = in IF part.
540	IF E < F THEN IF F > G THEN 550	Valid. If both conditions are satisfied, program goes to line 550.
550	IF A$<> "YES" THEN 540	Valid. If A$ is not equal to "YES," then program goes to line 540.

	Command	Comment
560	IF B = C = D THEN 570	Invalid. Only one relational operator is allowed per IF.
570	IF B$ = 101 THEN 560	Invalid. Strings must be enclosed in quotation marks. 101 is read as an integer, which is the wrong data type for B$ (string).
580	IF A <= C THEN LET C = A*(E/A)	Valid.

The other major command sequence used in the process block of a BASIC program is the FOR-NEXT sequence. There is no assembler instruction equivalent to this sequence, although a combination of instructions can be made to accomplish the same thing. The FOR-NEXT command sequence is used when a procedure must be repeated a known number of times. The FOR command gives the number of times the "loop" is to be repeated. The NEXT command signifies the end of the loop. The format of the FOR command is the three-character word FOR followed by an integer variable name; the equals operator; an integer, constant, or mathematical expression (that resolves to an integer); the two-letter word to; and another constant, integer, or mathematical expression. The format of the NEXT statement is simply the four-letter word NEXT followed by the name of the integer variable referenced in the FOR command. All valid lines between the FOR and NEXT commands will be repeated a number of times equal to the result of the second expression, variable, or constant of the FOR, minus the first expression, variable, or constant. Some examples of valid and invalid FOR-NEXT command sequences are:

	Command	Comment
600	FOR A = 1 to 10	Valid. Final value of B is 10 (if B was zero initially).
610	Let B = B+1	
620	NEXT A	
700	FOR B = 1 to 100	Invalid. Depending on the system, this will either iterate (repeat) one time or generate an error message immediately. The "loop variable" (B) must not be modified within its own loop.
710	LET B = B + 100	
720	NEXT B	
800	FOR C = (7 * D) to (E ** 2)	Valid if D and E are integers. Note that D and E are evaluated only once and the result of this evaluation replaces the expressions in the computer. Further modifications are allowed but may confuse the programmer.
810	LET D = D * .5	
820	LET E = E + 1	
830	LET F = E + D	
840	NEXT C	

Command	Comment
900 FOR Y = 20 to 30	Invalid. The NEXT Y command is in the wrong
910 FOR X = 1 to 10	place. If a loop is "nested" as in this example,
920 B = B + 1	the inner loop must be completed first. If 930
930 NEXT Y	said NEXT X and 940 said NEXT Y, the final
940 NEXT X	result of B would be B+100.

The PRINT command is the primary command used in an output block. This command causes the printer or cathode ray terminal to present information on the screen or on paper, depending on the device connected. The format of the command is the five-character word PRINT followed by a string in quotation marks, a variable, a constant, a number, or a mathematical expression. In the case of a string, all the material between quotes is printed exactly as it appears. The values of variables or constants are presented rather than their names.

Syntax errors (i.e., errors in the format of commands) are generally handled by routines in the compiler or interpreter. These routines usually disrupt the program, terminating program execution. Some BASIC interpreters allow an ONERR statement to intercede in error handling. In this case, the programmer is allowed to indicate how an error should be handled in order to avoid a system "crash." If recovery is possible through simple user intervention, data required from the user is solicited by routines in the error block. If input or calculations exceed an upper or lower limit that has been defined by the programmer, IF-THEN command sequences can be used to direct the program to the error-handling routines. These routines are customized by the programmer to fit the specifics of the program.

The END statement forms its own block, the end block. It simply indicates to the computer that the end of the program has been reached. Each program must contain at least one, preferably only one, END statement. The format of the END command is simply the three-character word END.

Variations of BASIC

Up to this point, only the "standard" BASIC commands have been discussed. Unfortunately, there is no "official" standard for BASIC. In fact, there is a great deal of variety in the command repertoire and syntax in BASIC compilers and interpreters marketed today. For this reason, a programmer must consult the documentation provided with a given interpreter or compiler before attempting to write programs with it.

The core commands that have been discussed are probably valid in any compiler or interpreter product currently available, but the way in which variables can be named differs widely from product to product. Some products allow any number of characters to be used in a variable name;

others restrict the user to two characters. Handling of files and matrixes that are not incorporated directly into the program (i.e., with READ and DATA commands) also varies considerably. With some products, data can be read from a matrix stored on a mass memory device simply by giving the name of the matrix, the row number, and the column number. With others, the entire matrix must be loaded into memory and checked by the program. Special commands for the calculation of trigonometric and other mathematical quantities (e.g., nth root of a number, numeric value of a string variable), may be used on some products.

MORE ABOUT LANGUAGE

Three of the more popular other computer languages are FORTRAN, Pascal, and COBOL.

FORTRAN

Historically, the first compilers and interpreters were for FORTRAN. The name FORTRAN is derived from FORmula TRANslation. As such, it was designed with the mathematician and scientist in mind, since they were the first to make extensive use of computers. There are many similarities between BASIC and FORTRAN. In fact, BASIC was originally devised as a simplification of FORTRAN that would allow beginners to program more successfully. Like BASIC, FORTRAN has a LET command that allows mathematical manipulation of data within the program. The READ command is similar to the BASIC input command, but allows the programmer to specify the input device. The PRINT and WRITE commands have different syntax and allow selection of device, but they are similar to BASIC's PRINT command.

The programmer has more control over the exact format of output in FORTRAN. Format statements allow the programmer to describe symbolically such output characteristics as the placement of variables and rounding off of variables. FORTRAN has GOTO command as BASIC does, but FORTRAN lines require a line number only if a GOTO command makes reference to them. GOSUB is present as the CALL command. Instead of a line number, a subroutine name is "called." Subroutines are created and defined by the word Subroutine. IF-THEN is a valid command sequence in FORTRAN; however, program loops are handled differently in FORTRAN. The syntax is DO I = J,K 200, where I is a loop-counting variable, K is the limit of the looping, and 200 is the line number that terminates the program loop. The FORTRAN program repeats every statement between the DO statement and the numbered statement referenced for a number of times equal to K − J. FORTRAN allows not only subroutines, but also user definition of FUNCTIONS. By using a FUNCTION command sequence, the programmer can create mathematical operators that are not part of standard FORTRAN. For example, a user may repeatedly need to know the value of a number factorial divided by itself: N!/N. With FORTRAN, it is possible to define an operator that performs this operation. Naming of variables and many minor details of syntax are also differences between BASIC and FORTRAN.

FORTRAN is primarily useful for purely mathematical programming. Its handling of data structures, especially strings, is less efficient. Several microcomputers and virtually all large computers have FORTRAN products available to them. Several of the FORTRAN compilers used on larger systems are said to produce object code that is as efficient as, if not more efficient than, object code written by human assembly language programmers. FORTRAN may excel in pharmacy applications such as pharmacokinetic analysis, statistical analysis of management or patient data, and calculation of ingredients for complex total parenteral nutrition formulations.

Pascal

Professor Niklaus Wirth, credited with the development of the Pascal language, chose to name the language after the thirteenth century French mathematician and religious philosopher Blaise Pascal. Figure 2–5 illustrates the syntax of the Pascal language. These diagrams are actually an excellent example of the concept of levels of abstraction. They are presented in order here from highest to lowest level of abstraction. The first level (Figure 2–5, a) describes the total structure of a Pascal program. To interpret these diagrams, the lines should always be followed in the direction indicated by the arrowhead. If the line branches, either path may be followed, depending on what the program is supposed to do. Lower case words in squared boxes are either self-explanatory or an abstraction that is further defined by another diagram. Upper case words in rounded boxes and punctuation in circles are literal parts of the syntax of Pascal. These must appear in a program exactly as indicated for the program to function correctly.

As shown in Figure 2–5, a Pascal program must be composed of the word PROGRAM followed by an identifier, open parenthesis, one or more identifiers separated by commas, closed parenthesis, a semicolon, a block, and a period. Like a sentence, a Pascal program ends with a period. The identifiers between parentheses describe external files to be used by the

Figure 2-5 Pascal Syntax

a) program

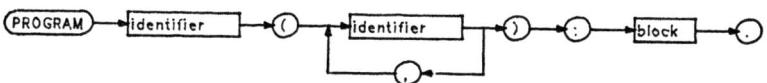

b) block

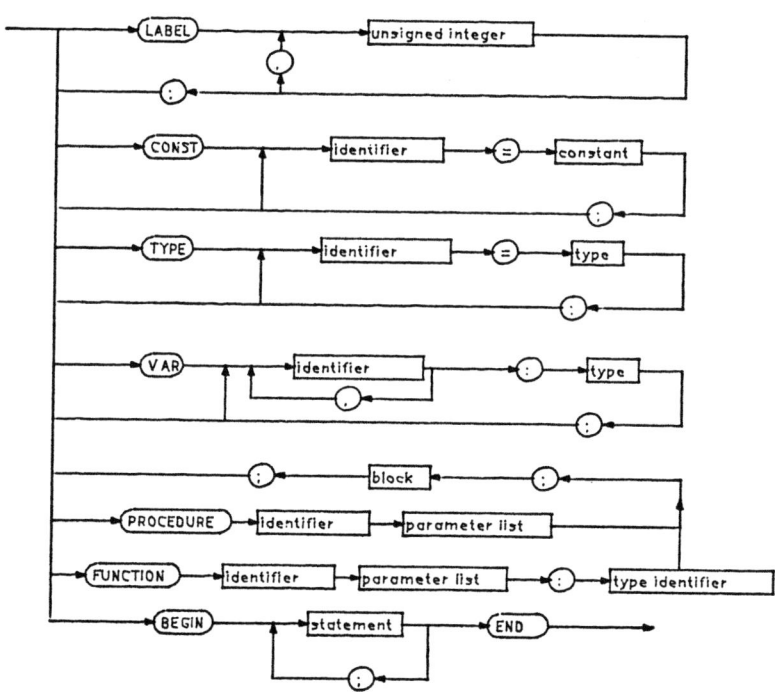

Figure 2–5 continued

c) statement

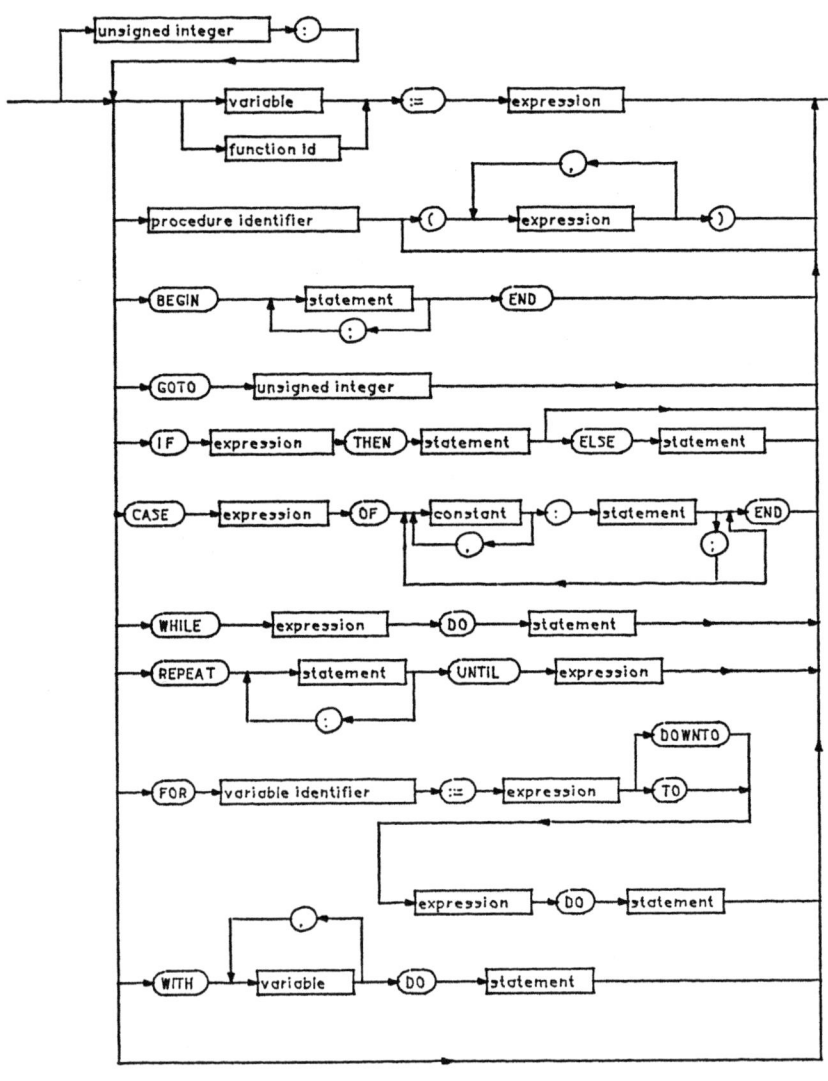

Figure 2–5 continued

d) parameter list

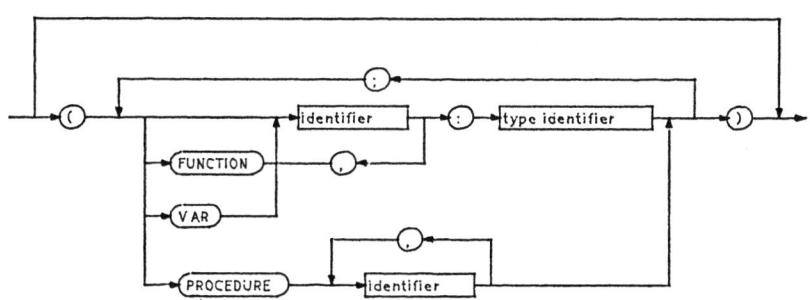

e) expression

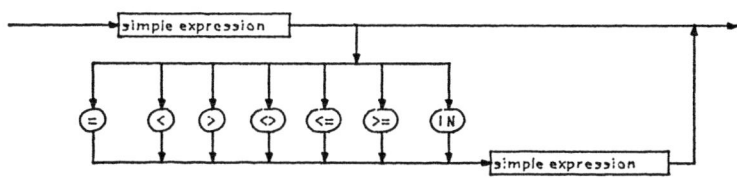

f) simple expression

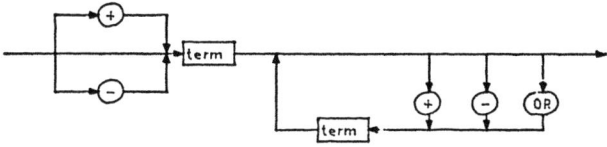

g) term

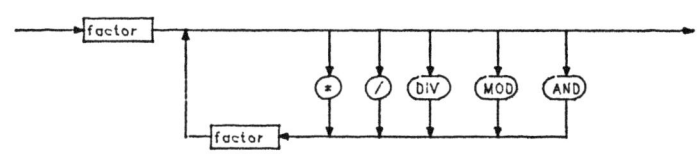

Figure 2–5 continued

h) factor

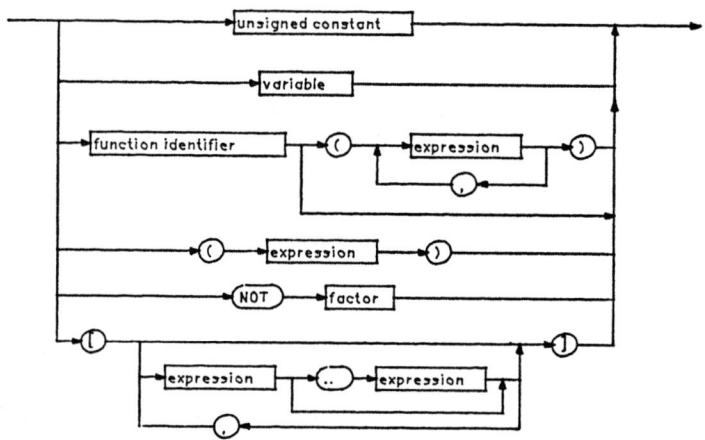

i) variable

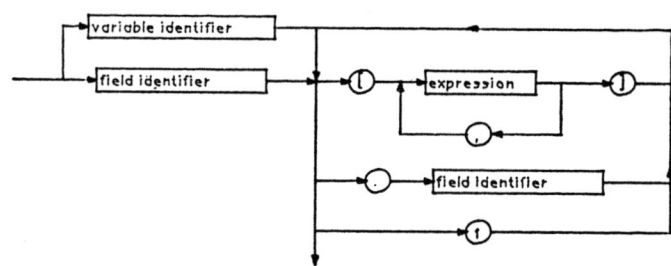

j) field list

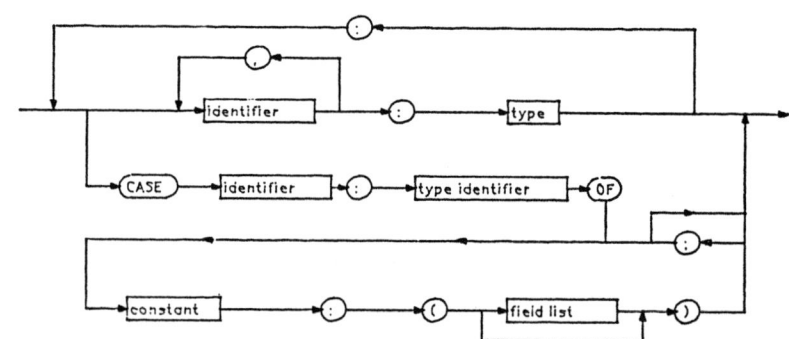

Figure 2–5 continued

k) type

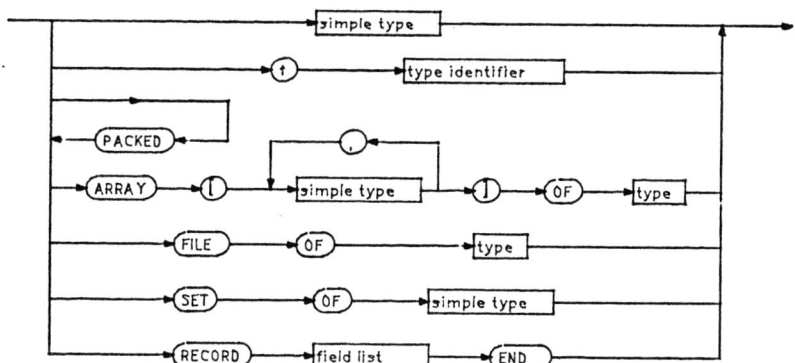

l) simple type

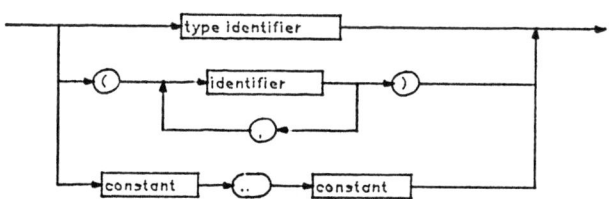

m) constant

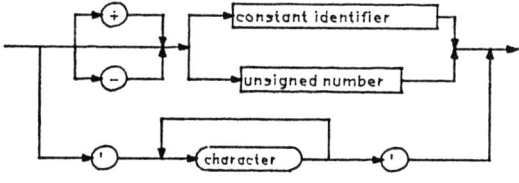

n) unsigned constant

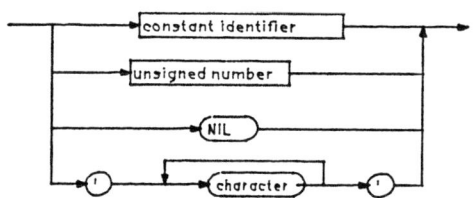

Figure 2-5 continued

o) unsigned number

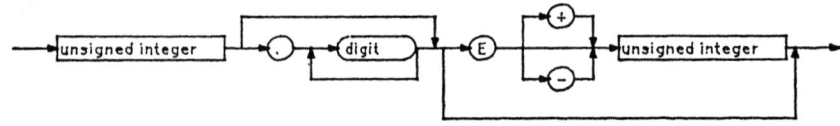

p) unsigned integer

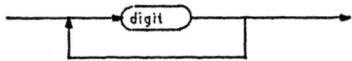

q) identifier

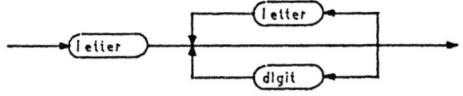

program. It is commonly necessary to define two special files—input and output—so that the computer knows to accept input from the keyboard and to send output to the video display.

A block is defined in Figure 2-5, b. The only part of a block that is explicitly required is the word BEGIN, a statement, and the word END. In actual practice, however, a block that contained only this could never be written because Pascal requires definition of every constant, variable, and data structure element before it is used. The words CONST, TYPE, and VAR define sub-blocks associated with data structure definition. The identifiers contain the mnemonic associated with each data structure element. CONST and TYPE describe the element's usage. It is essential that the parts appear in the order given. LABEL is used to define statement numbers that make use of GOTO statements. PROCEDURE and FUNC-

TION allow definition of subroutines and user-defined functions, respectively.

The definition of statement is presented in Figure 2–5, c. All of the possible Pascal commands are indicated in upper case. A statement may begin with an unsigned integer if it will be the object of a GOTO statement. The assignment operator := (colon followed by an equals sign) is shown as acting on a variable or a function identifier and an expression. The next option shown, although it need not be in this order in a program, is to call a procedure. This is done very simply in Pascal by giving its name (the procedure identifier that follows PROCEDURE in Figure 2–5, a) and the names of the data structure elements on which the procedure is to operate. Called expressions, these elements appear in parentheses following the procedure name and can become quite complex. The next option shows that a statement may be composed of any number of statements by using BEGIN and END, but a semicolon must separate each statement. The next option demonstrates how to use GOTO, the unconditional branching construct. Conditional branching is allowed via IF-THEN statements, as in BASIC and FORTRAN. However, Pascal allows explicit definition of the action to be taken if the expression evaluates to false by providing the optional word ELSE followed by a statement. If the ELSE option is not used and the IF statement evaluates to false, the program proceeds with the statement following the IF statement. The CASE construct allows conditional branching to one of several statements based on the value of an expression, usually a variable. If the expression does not correspond to any of the constants specified, the statement following the CASE construct is followed. CASE therefore acts like a series of IF expression = constant THEN statements.

Pascal has three kinds of looping statements. The first two repeat an operation until an expression becomes true. These are WHILE-DO and REPEAT-UNTIL. Because the REPEAT has the statement(s) before the expression, the statement(s) will always be executed at least one time, even if the expression is true at the time the loop is started. With the WHILE construct, in contrast, the statement will not be executed at all if the expression is not true when the loop is entered. The FOR-DO loop is very similar to BASIC's FOR-NEXT loop. If the number of iterations is known ahead of time and never varies, this is the looping control construct to use. Pascal differs from BASIC in that only one statement (which may be composed of several by using BEGIN and END) is executed by the loop. WITH allows simple handling of complex data structures.

Basically, a parameter list (Figure 2–5, d) identifies the structure of the data being passed into and out of a procedure. Procedures or functions that are used within a procedure must also be declared in the parameter list. An expression (Figure 2-5, e) may be either a simple expression or a relationship between two simple expressions. The relational operators are self-explanatory. IN means the expression is part of a set described by the second expression. If this is true, the expression evaluates to true or 1. Otherwise, it gives 0 or false. A simple expression (Figure 2-5, f) may consist of as little as a term, or it may consist of a logical relationship between several terms. A term (Figure 2-5, g) may consist of as little as a single factor, or it may consist of a mathematical relationship between a series of factors. A factor (Figure 2-5, h) may consist of a simple unsigned constant or variable, or it may consist of a function identifier with or without an expression in parentheses. A factor may be an entire expression or a range between two expressions between square brackets. It may include the word NOT to express the opposite of the normal evaluation of the factor.

A variable (Figure 2-5, i) must begin with either a variable identifier or a field identifier. It may also include an expression or definition of complex data structures. The variable identifier must correspond to a variable defined in the program. The field identifier must correspond to an identifier defined in a field list (Figure 2-5, j). A field list is used to define the type of variables, functions, and records. The use of CASE in a field list allows definition of complex variant data structures that vary according to the actual content of related data structures.

Type (Figure 2-5, k) defines to the computer what kind of information is stored in the data structure element. It may be simple, or it may be complex, such as RECORD with its corresponding field list. The ↑ defines a special data type (see Chapter 5). PACKED types use less memory than nonpacked types, but they slow down the operation of the computer. Arrays may be of any type and can be indexed by any simple type. Thus, an array of records can be indexed by the letters of the alphabet. Likewise, an array of arrays of any type can be defined. The result is a matrix of that type. Several indexes, separated by commas, may be specified between the square brackets of the array definition. Usually, the degree or number of dimensions of the matrix is limited only by the memory available. Simple type is defined in Figure 2-5, l. Type identifier refers to any of the predefined variable types, such as CHAR, REAL, and INTEGER. Simple type may also consist of a series of literal identifiers separated by commas and enclosed in parentheses. Even a range of values between two constants may be used to define a type.

A constant (Figure 2-5, m) may be defined in terms of another constant, using its identifier, an unsigned number, or a series of characters enclosed in single quotation marks. A plus or minus sign may precede numeric constants. The main difference between unsigned constants (Figure 2-5,

n) and signed constants is the lack of plus and minus signs and the definition of the standard constant NIL, which has a value of 0. Definitions of unsigned number (Figure 2–5, o), unsigned integer (Figure 2–5, p), and identifier (Figure 2–5, q) are straightforward. Identifiers must start with a letter, but may include digits or letters in the remainder of the name.

Appendix D presents a Pascal program equivalent to the BASIC program of Appendix C. It is much easier to understand than the BASIC version. Pascal was developed after the value of modular, structured programming had been recognized, and the organization of a Pascal program is such that it assumes the programmer will use a structured modular style. One important feature of Pascal is that it is self-documenting—the statements of Pascal are sufficiently English-like that few purely documenting statements need to be written. In Pascal, records, matrixes, and files can be named with complex fixed or variable field length definitions, much as variables are named in other languages. This greatly facilitates the implementation of efficient data structures. One drawback of Pascal is that the set of mathematical operators usually available is relatively limited. For this reason, some critics have claimed that Pascal is poorly suited to mathematical programs (where FORTRAN excels). The majority of users would probably disagree with this opinion, believing instead that this lack is more than overcome by Pascal's ability to accept user-defined functions either in Pascal or in object code.

Pascal is currently experiencing a surge of popularity. Most large computer systems and several microcomputers now offer Pascal compiler or interpreter products. The University of California at San Diego has developed a Pascal compiler that converts programs written in Pascal into a file similar to an object code called a P-code file. P-code mnemonics are like a hypothetical computer's object code. Each 16-bit code has a specific meaning. In order to use this compiler on a given computer, all that needs to be written is an assembly level program that "interprets" the P-code generated by the compiler. By taking this approach, the University of California at San Diego has effectively made a standard Pascal language system (monitor, compiler, text editor, linker, assembler) available for a wide variety of microcomputer systems. One computer system has even been built so that its assembly object codes are the P-codes generated by this compiler. This is an unusual situation in which hardware was designed to fit software.

COBOL

As indicated by the fact that its name is derived from COmmon Business Oriented Language, COBOL is a business oriented language with facilities that make it ideal for handling large files and large volumes of input and output. Its commands make text formatting and modification easier. Although mathematical manipulation is possible with COBOL, the English-like organization of the commands makes COBOL inefficient for this application. COBOL requires a block format. It has a standard format that is officially recognized by the American National Standards Institute (ANSI). COBOL products that adhere to this standard are commonly referred to as ANSI standard COBOL. COBOL programs tend to be verbose, as compared to those written in FORTRAN, BASIC, or Pascal. For this reason, they are not often used on microcomputers with small memory areas. Virtually all larger computer systems and a few small computer systems have a COBOL product available, however. Pharmacy applications for which COBOL might be used include patient billing and accounting, promotional mailing list manipulation, and patient profile handling.

Chapter 3

Computer Components: Input, Output, and Storage Devices

3

A large number of machines have been devised to provide an interface between computers and the real world. The cost of such equipment is subject to two opposing forces. As technology becomes more advanced, parts become smaller and, usually, less expensive. As equipment becomes less expensive, however, the number of applications in which it is cost-effective to use a computer increases. This greatly increases the demand for equipment, resulting in a seller's market.

There is more to be considered in buying computer equipment than price and capabilities. There are other primary considerations: dependability, serviceability, and expandability. Dependability is the hardest consideration to quantify. Without a thorough understanding of digital equipment design, the average buyer cannot judge dependability, although it can sometimes be judged by appearance and the warranty. A given brand name does not necessarily indicate the level of dependability. The second consideration, serviceability, should possibly come first. What is to be done when (not if) this equipment breaks down? Is there a local service organization? Do they make "house" calls? Are loaners available? What is the average repair turnaround time? Is it possible to obtain a written guarantee of repair turnaround time? There is a vast difference between this and a warranty; with a warranty, the equipment could conceivably, within its terms, be out of operation for a month or more. With a properly executed repair contract, it is reasonably certain that the equipment will be functioning within the specified amount of time. Expandability is the ability of the equipment to accept modifications that increase its capabilities without costing an exorbitant amount. It must be possible to expand the system as the organization it serves expands. Otherwise, the cost of a small incremental growth could conceivably equal the cost of the initial system.

A final general criterion for equipment selection should be software (programs) availability. In some cases, a hardware system is purchased solely on the basis of the availability of programs (i.e., turnkey or prefabricated vended pharmacy systems). Availability of system software (e.g., compilers, interpreters) and prepackaged programs in the field of interest can save significantly in development costs. This effectively modifies the cost of the equipment by reducing life cycle cost of the overall system.

MAINFRAMES

The term *mainframe* is actually a carry over from the days when the central processing unit (CPU) was mounted in a large metal frame. In this context, the mainframe consisted of the components (e.g., vacuum tubes, transistors) that formed the CPU. Everything else was considered a "peripheral." As components became smaller and smaller, more and more of the peripheral equipment came to be part of the metal frame (mainframe). Today, the term has come to mean the CPU plus all the components that are on the same circuit board and are not designed for easy connection and disconnection. Available systems range from a complete collection of all the parts necessary to start functioning to a CPU and connectors to attach the rest of the system.

Aside from the number of peripherals and peripheral slots (connectors) included in a mainframe, the item of primary importance is the CPU. CPUs are judged primarily by speed, which is roughly proportional to the word size. A statistic sometimes used in evaluating CPUs is million instructions per second (mips). This is simply the maximum, minimum, or average (depending on how quoted) number of millions of instructions the CPU can perform per second consistently. When word size is equal, mips is roughly proportional to the clock speed (measured in megahertz, i.e., millions of cycles per second). Of course, a million instructions on one CPU do not necessarily perform as much of a given type of work as a million instructions on another CPU. Differences in the architecture of CPUs favor certain types of applications over others. For this reason, a benchmark program is sometimes written. The benchmark program causes the system to perform repeatedly a set of instructions that are believed to be typical of the instructions to be used in the application. The time taken to perform the benchmark program is then taken as an indication of the relative speed of the CPU in the given application.

Another major consideration in the choice of CPU is the address space. The address space or addressing range of a CPU is the amount of memory it can directly address at one time. The address range is directly determined by the number of lines or bits on the address bus. Most 8-bit processors have a 16-bit address bus, meaning that they can directly address 2^{16} (65,536) bytes of memory. Some system engineers have attempted to overcome this limitation by placing memory in banks that are switched on and off by a specific CPU instruction. This is really only a partial solution, however, because not all the data in memory can be used at the same time. Sixteen-bit CPUs commonly have address buses exceeding 20 bits and so can generally address around one megabyte (2^{20} = 1,048,576 bytes) of memory directly. On larger systems, addressing range is not usually an issue, because it is very large.

The amount of software generally available in the specific object code of the CPU is also a significant consideration. If a processor has only recently been introduced, it is not likely to have a great deal of system software available unless the new processor is an extension of an old one and accepts object code generated for the previous model. In this instance, the old object code may not run optimally on the new processor, however.

INFORMATION STORAGE DEVICES

Most information storage devices cannot be used interchangeably from one computer system to another. For example, random access memory (RAM) chips must be of the correct type to be plugged into a computer circuit. Disk drives and tape drives must be interfaced to the mainframe by a controller specifically designed to work with that mainframe. Furthermore, a given controller controls only one specific type of drive, and a drive is usually sold with the controller to fit a specified mainframe. It can generally be assumed that the controller is compatible with system software produced by the manufacturer of the mainframe. However, system software produced by another vendor may not necessarily be compatible.

Semiconductor Memory

There are several basic types of semiconductor memory, including RAM, read only memory (ROM), and erasable programmable ROM (EPROM). In addition, there are two types of RAM, dynamic and static. Dynamic RAM slowly loses its information (over a few milliseconds) and therefore must be refreshed periodically. Refreshing dynamic memories slows the CPU, resulting in a slower overall system. Static RAM never loses its contents while turned on, but it is more expensive. It behooves the buyer to make sure that the word size of a memory device under consideration is the same as the size of the data bus of the system with which it is to be used.

ROMs are usually programmed en masse and sold on the basis of their contents rather than size. They are also very specific as to the configuration of peripherals required. Often they work only within a specific product marketed by the manufacturer who programs them. EPROM circuits are available in two basic types, those that program EPROMs and those that merely provide access for reading them. Semiconductor memory is the fastest but most expensive type of information storage device currently available.

Ferrite Core Memory

Commonly referred to as core memory, ferrite core memory is very similar in operation to static RAM, but it is constructed as a series of magnetic toroids (donut-shaped magnets) strung on crossed wires. One set of wires is used to magnetize (set) the toroids by sending an electric current through them; the other set is used to read the information by measuring the toroids' effect on a lower current passed through them. Construction of such memory is more difficult than that of semiconductor memory. The core is not volatile.

Tape

Magnetic tape, in one form or another, has been the workhorse of information storage almost since the beginning of the computer era. In fact, cinema set designers, magazine illustrators, and others who wish to picture a computer usually, although mistakenly, show one or several tape drives. Although tape and tape drives are currently the least expensive information storage devices for large quantities of information, their sequential nature renders them slower than other devices. All sequential devices have the disadvantage that, if information is needed from one end and the tape happens to be at the other end, the entire tape must be advanced. This takes inordinate amounts of time. For this reason, sequential devices are rarely used in information search applications. Random access devices, which can skip over a great deal of information, are used instead. Tape is used, however, when speed of access is not of prime concern (e.g., archival storage).

Virtually every type of magnetic tape yet invented has been used to store data from a computer, including the small C type cassettes. The real workhorse of the industry is the reel of ½-inch tape. Large tape drives are available mainly for large computer systems, although several devices interfaced to microcomputers are beginning to appear. Cassette interfaces for standard C cassettes commonly use standard cassette recorders.

Disks

Information can also be stored on disks, which are flat, circular, magnetized devices. In use, they are spun at high rates of speed and accessed by a magnetic pick up (head) that can either read or store information. They are random access devices since the head can skip over several tracks (concentric circles in which data are stored) to reach the track with the desired information on it. They are very fast, but relatively expensive. They are used mainly when speed of access is a primary consideration. There are three basic types of disk drive.

One type of disk drive accepts portable flexible diskettes (referred to as floppies or floppy diskettes). These diskettes are of two sizes. The 5¼ inch can hold about 500,000 bytes, and the 8 inch can hold as many as 1 million bytes, depending on the design of the drive. Another type of disk drive has no removable parts, and its magnetic surface is an alloy of high-quality steel. The capacity of this type of device may range from 10 megabytes (10^6 bytes) to 250 megabytes. The final type of disk is the cartridge disk drive, which has a hard-surfaced removable platter. Capacity of these devices is basically the same as that of the nonremovable ones.

The advantage of cartridge disks is that they allow a backup copy of data or programs to be made very rapidly and efficiently. Backup copies of data from the permanent platter devices are usually made on tape, requiring the purchase of tape drive and controller and usually taking far more time.

Advantages of the floppy disk are low cost and virtually unlimited library size. Only a small portion of a library is on-line at a given time, however, and floppy diskettes are susceptible to damage from normal use (bending them can cause loss of data and programs). Although permanent platter disk drives have the advantages of a more rapid retrieval rate and greater permanency of data, they also have higher unit costs. Furthermore, the library size is limited to that which is on-line. The advantage of cartridge (removable platter) disk drives is the quick backup automatically available. Otherwise, these drives are basically the same as the permanent platter drives.

Storage Devices of the Future

Several new storage devices are expected to come into widespread use within five years, along with a couple of unconventional uses of existing technologies to store information.

Bubble Memory

A rapid sequential information storage form, bubble memory utilizes charged bubbles circulating around wire loops. Currently available devices can store 250,000 bits of information at a cost roughly equivalent to that of a floppy disk drive. Cost of bubble memory devices is expected to drop substantially, to the point that they compete with other devices. Bubble memories are nonvolatile. Physical size of these devices is much smaller than that of currently available floppy disk drives.

Optical Disks

Also known as video disks, optical disks are the same devices used to store and play movies for television. Basically, the medium is a reflective or translucent 12-inch disk that contains analog information in the form of greater or lesser reflectance or translucence on its surface. The disk is spun at high speed, and a laser is used to read the amount of light reflected or passing through. Digital information can be recorded on these disks and interpreted by specially designed computer circuits. At present, these devices are still experimental; the reliability of data storage is not yet completely acceptable. The capacity of currently available disks is approximately 14 gigabits (14×10^9 bits). This is equivalent to the information content of, for example, several sets of encyclopedias.

There are currently two obstacles to the widespread use of video disks. A digital controller must be developed, and the devices so far being manufactured are read only machines. The process of writing on video disks is very similar to that of making phonograph records, except that a videotape is used as a master, rather than an audio tape. Since video disks cannot be erased, it is unlikely that they will ever be used for anything other than archival storage. They may, however, change the face of the information publishing industry, as smaller, hand-held read and display devices may be designed to use subpocket-sized disks, which could be marketed as books are today.

Mark Sense and Optical Characters

Two currently well-developed technologies that are not traditionally associated with information storage are mark sense forms and optical characters. Those examinations in which boxes are filled in with a pencil and read by a computer device are the most familiar mark sense forms. Optical characters are any characters that can be read by an optical character reader. Writing to these media can be manual, mechanical, or automatic. Manual writing is done with a pencil, as in the case of mark sense forms.

Mechanical writing is done with a typewriter equipped with an optical character recognition (OCR) font. Automatic writing is done with an on-line computer printer equipped with an OCR font.

The advantages of this storage medium are that the material is easily read both by humans and by machines and that printed information sometimes satisfies legal requirements (e.g., controlled substance records) that magnetic media do not. Input to these media is also more flexible. On the other hand, the readers are relatively slow and the information is not on-line. A human must feed the appropriate documents for conversion to an on-line medium before the information can be processed. Mark sense and OCR devices are most satisfactory for archival or backup storage of information. The medium (paper) is about the least expensive storage medium used in the industry. The cost of OCR readers varies depending on whether they turn pages automatically and what they do when they encounter an illegible character.

INPUT DEVICES

Information may be entered into computers by devices as simple as a set of switches or as complex as television cameras. The input device is required to put the information into an electronic format that can be directly used by the mainframe. Usually, this is done by means of a communication standard between the input device and the mainframe. To determine whether a given input device from one manufacturer is compatible with a mainframe from another manufacturer, it is usually necessary to determine only if both use the same communication standard. Some input devices are sold with interfaces specifically designed for several popular mainframes. In these instances, it is necessary to specify on which mainframe the device will be used when ordering.

Cathode Ray Terminals

Sometimes referred to as cathode ray tubes because they share an abbreviation—CRT—cathode ray terminals are the primary type of input device used today. These terminals are composed of a cathode ray tube (television screen), a keyboard, and at least one communication port. Some less expensive devices have no screen but, rather, transmit the display to the antenna terminals of a standard television set by means of a cable. Some mainframes have a "bare minimum" terminal in the form of a keyboard directly interfaced to the CPU. This type of mainframe usually also has a radio frequency modulated output that displays information through a standard television. The number of keys varies from the "standard" 53 to over 75. The inclusion of extra keys, such as a calculator style numeric key pad, is considered a quality feature.

CRTs usually generate only one information code, such as the American Standard Code for Information Interchange (ASCII). The user must ensure that the software, both system and application, to be used recognizes the character code of the input device to be used. Some terminals allow entry of both upper and lower case alphabetic characters, while others do not. This is another quality-determining feature.

CRTs are usually classified as intelligent or dumb. Intelligent terminals are characterized by a microcomputer controller, memory, and built-in text-editing features. Actually, a mainframe with interfaced keyboard and a communication port can be used as an intelligent terminal with appropriate programming. Dumb terminals have fewer features, but usually cost less.

Printing Terminals

The major difference between a CRT and a printing terminal is that the printing terminal displays output on paper rather than on a television screen. Printing terminals cost more than CRTs, and their upkeep (paper cost) is also higher. Most printing terminals can also be used as printers, being driven by a mainframe. Printing terminals are not usually as intelligent as CRTs, and, because they are mechanical, they are not capable of high-speed communication.

Other Input Devices

There are several other less conventional or less frequently used input devices. For example, card readers, primarily used to read punched card data and programs, are in use mainly on larger, older computers. Paper tape readers, which read perforated paper tape, are also in use mainly on larger, older computers.

Optical Character Readers

OCR equipment may be used to input data that has been printed on paper by means of one of the many OCR fonts available. The development of the Xerox Corporation's Kurzweil machine promises to render virtually all printed material readable by OCR equipment. When this occurs, the distinction between print publishing and on-line publishing will diminish. This should make information more accessible to users, but it is bound to have profound implications on the economics of publishing.

Video Digitizers

Devices that interface a television camera to a computer are video digitizers. Televisions work by presenting a matrix of white, gray (or color), and black dots on the screen very close together. The human eye interprets these dots as a picture. A television camera has a device in it that converts a light image (a reflection) into a matrix of higher and lower voltage signals. Video digitizers convert these higher and lower voltages to binary bits that can be interpreted by a computer. This technique might be applied to the optical character reader by focusing a television camera on some print and giving it instructions on how to interpret the alphabet, for example. Another primary application of this technology is robotics. A robot that fastens bolts to the chassis of a car is taught what the bolt looks like, what the car looks like, and how to position the two in proper relation to the automatic wrench.

Analog to Digital Interfaces

Commonly called A/D devices, analogs to digital interfaces convert an analog signal, such as the voltage across a heat-sensing resistor, into digital information that can be used by a computer. In fact, an A/D device is what a video digitizer uses to create its matrix of binary information. The primary use of A/D devices is in the control of industrial processes. A device converts the property to be controlled (e.g., pressure) into a proportional voltage (e.g., pressure transducer). This voltage is converted to binary information, which is periodically evaluated by the computer. If the numeric value of this information exceeds a predetermined control value, the computer activates a mechanism that corrects the excess. A/D converters are also used in control of domestic devices, such as solar energy heating systems. Animal pharmacology laboratories are increasingly using these devices to reduce personnel needs, as well as the chance for human error, in making measurements during drug testing.

Graphics Tablets

Pressure-sensitive writing surfaces, graphics tablets capture a binary pattern by giving the Cartesian coordinates (x and y points) of whatever is drawn on them. They have many uses in drafting and drawing industries. An obvious use of such a device in a pharmacy would be to capture, transmit, or store such items as authorization signatures on prescriptions. A file of authorization signatures might be compiled for verification of the authenticity of prescriptions. The cost of graphics tablets varies greatly according to size and resolution (number of points in 1 inch).

Voice Input

Although their use is somewhat limited now, voice input devices that recognize as many as 64 different words or phrases are currently available. These devices are calibrated by saying the word or phrase and typing in the digitally equivalent word or phrase. The word or phrase must then be repeated until the device recognizes it. Voice input devices recognize only one person's voice and may need recalibrating if that person gets a cold.

OUTPUT DEVICES

Computers present information to humans by means of output devices. In fact, the basic difference between an output device and a storage device is that the output device prepares material that is human-readable, whereas the storage device prepares material that is machine-readable. This distinction is beginning to vanish, however, as machines are being taught to read human compatible material.

Printers

Printers are the workhorses of the computer output business. As such, a large number of devices that make legible marks on paper or paperlike substances have been developed. The primary quality criteria for printers are speed, legibility, permanence, paper type, noise, and character set.

Speed is important for obvious reasons. The faster it will print, the more work it can do. Legibility is related to the subjective appearance of the material produced. Appearance would seem to be more important in trying to make a good impression on a new business prospect than in producing routine managerial reports within a company. The permanence of the image on the paper or paperlike substance is primarily an issue with certain types of chemically treated paper that discolor with age. The paper type that the machine requires or will accept is especially important if the printer is to be left unattended. In this case, it is essential that the printer accept pinfeed paper to ensure continued alignment of paper or forms. Availability of printed forms for the printer model (standard or custom designed) is also a consideration.

Noise is a consideration when the printer will be operating where people are working. Under Occupational Safety and Health Administration guidelines, ear protectors must be issued to employees if noise exceeds a specified level. Excessive noise is unhealthful and, in most instances, decreases productivity and morale of employees. It is not, as some manufacturers imply, a minor problem. Obviously, printers to be used in patient care areas must be silent.

The character set required of a printer depends on the planned use of the output. Early models of computer printers had only one character set—upper case alphabet, numbers, and punctuation. People came to identify computer output as squared off and all upper case. This is not always the case, however. For correspondence or just plain communication, both upper and lower case, as well as special characters, are available.

Printers require an output port from the mainframe to drive them. Because the configuration of this port varies significantly from printer to printer, it is usually necessary to purchase a specific printer controller for a given printer. When the printer functions as part of a printing terminal, however, some standard interfaces are available.

Formed Font Impact Printers

The printers that produce a legible image by striking an inked ribbon and a piece of paper with a font shaped like the character to be represented are called formed font impact printers. A typewriter is a manual formed font impact printer. Several models of formed font printer are, in fact, modified typewriters. Formed font printers are available with and without keyboard, although the former are really printing terminals. Formed font printers are relatively slow, owing to the high momentum of the mechanically moving fonts. They compensate by producing extremely legible characters that are generally as permanent as the paper on which they are printed. These printers usually accept any paper that a typewriter will accept. Some devices have pinfeed mechanisms. In addition, these devices, like most impact printers, usually handle multiple copy forms quite well. Unfortunately, the very force of their impact causes these devices to be quite noisy, especially when they operate at higher speeds. Almost without variation, these machines have upper and lower case symbols, often with the option of interchanging the font element to achieve a different type face or character set.

Dot Matrix Impact Printers

The operation of dot matrix impact printers involves striking an inked ribbon and the paper with a pin or an array of pins. Characters are formed by placing the dots thus printed in a matrix or pattern that looks like the character desired. Since the size and mass of the print "pin" is much smaller than that of a formed font, dot matrix printers are generally capable of somewhat higher speeds than formed font devices. However, legibility may suffer. The matrix size of these machines is the primary determinant of their legibility. The most common matrix size is five dots across by seven dots down.

The permanence of dot matrix output is the same as that of the paper used, and there are dot matrix printers that use almost every type of paper available. The predominant type has a pinfeed mechanism attached. As they are impact printers, these printers also work quite well with multiple copy forms. Unfortunately, they are quite noisy, although not usually as noisy as formed font machines. A major advantage of some models of these machines is the availability of a variety of characters. Because these models allow the computer to have complete control over the print pins and the print head position, any character set desired may be produced with properly written programs. In fact, these printers may be used to draw graphs, pictures, or other illustrations and to intermix these with characters. Their drawback in this mode is that the resolution, in terms of dots per inch, is somewhat limited (60 to 120 dots per inch).

Dot Matrix Electrostatic Printers

In order to form an image on a paperlike substance, dot matrix electrostatic printers discharge an electric spark through the substance. The paperlike substance may be chemically treated paper or a composite of thin aluminum foil and paper. These printers operate at a relatively high speed. The characters formed are as legible as those of any other dot matrix printer, except that the contrast between the chemically treated or aluminized background is not as high (generally) as that between black ink and white paper. This may cause problems if photocopies are desired. The images produced by these printers are the least permanent of any of the printers discussed, because chemically treated papers are particularly prone to discoloration. This severely limits the usefulness of this type of printer for any record-keeping function. These printers are usually designed around a single paper type, and no forms or carbon copies are possible. They are relatively noiseless, as there is no impact. The character sets available on dot matrix electrostatic printers are virtually the same as those available on dot matrix impact printers, including graphics and other options. These printers are among the least expensive.

Ink Jet Printers

By squirting ink from a series of small jets, ink jet printers produce an image on paper. The characters formed resemble dot matrix characters, but are usually a bit more legible. The speed of an ink jet printer is relatively high. The characters are as permanent as the paper, which may be almost any type of single thickness paper. The major selling point of these printers is that they are virtually noiseless and, thus, are considered acceptable for patient care areas. At present, there is only one manufacturer of an ink jet printer. This printer has upper and lower case characters, but no graphics.

Xerographic Printers

A relatively new development, xerographic printers produce their output by using a laser to place an image of what is to be printed onto the transfer drum of a modified xerographic photocopier. The drum then transfers the image onto standard xerographic paper by sealing carbon particles with heat. These are the fastest printers currently available. The characters are as legible as those produced by a good typewriter and as permanent as xerographic photocopy. Standard xerographic bond paper is the only type of paper that can be used. This printer is among the noisiest and largest of those discussed; it really belongs in some type of print shop or high-volume output printer arrangement. Its character set is extremely flexible, including several sizes and types of boldface shapes, graphics, and shading for forms design. Thus, it can print and fill in a form at the same time. New low-cost versions are soon expected to be priced similarly to photocopiers.

Plotters

Devices that draw pictures under computer control are called plotters. Basically, an A/D device connected to the computer controls motors connected to pens. The pens are positioned on paper and the computer controls the drawing of the picture. All of the figures in this book were produced by the author using a pen plotter connected to a time-sharing computer. Dot matrix printers that can draw pictures can be called plotters. Some dot matrix devices were designed primarily as plotters, although characters can obviously be "drawn" with them, albeit slowly. For a high-quality image, pen and ink plotters, available with as many as four concurrent colors produce the best illustration. These images are as permanent as the pen and ink used to create them. Electrostatic paper for those devices that require it is similar to that for printers except that it is larger for a plotter.

Video Devices

The image produced by video devices is not a permanent one that can be stored and retrieved manually. Video devices work on the basic principles of a television set. In fact, some computers use an unmodified television as a video output device. They do this by using a radio frequency modulator that generates a very low power version of the type of signal broadcast by television stations. The basic principle of a video screen is that an electron beam scans from left to right across a glass plate. When it hits the plate, a phosphor on the plate gives off light. The color of light given off is a function of the chemical nature of the phosphor. The electron beam is then successively turned on and off, resulting in a matrix of on and off dots. The beam moves so rapidly and the dots are so close together that the human eye interprets them as a moving picture.

Digital information to be displayed in this way is organized so as to create the pattern of the character or other illustration desired. Depending on the system being used, character, picture, animation, and other effects can be achieved; many of the special effects used in cinema are done in this way. Color video outputs probably enhance the communication of information, but there is some associated expense. When a printed copy of the information is not needed (which is most of the time), video output saves the cost of the paper and preserves trees.

Microforms

Microfiche, microfilm, and other reduced size output media that are not directly readable by the human eye but require high-power magnification devices to be read are called microforms. Microfiche, commonly called fiche or fish, is similar in appearance to a plastic index card, usually about 4 × 6 inches in size. Approximately 100 to 200 pages of material can be put on a single fiche. Microfilm looks like a roll of 16-mm or 35-mm movie film. Several thousand to several million pages can be put on a reel of microfilm. Clearly, the space and paper saved in both are quite significant. The access process is somewhat cumbersome, however, and some people do not like reading from the magnifying viewer.

It is not commonly appreciated how easy it is to produce microfiche. Some devices produce microfiche from computer tape. They are called computer output microfiche or COM devices (COM may also be used to denote the output of such a device). Although these devices are quite expensive, there are service bureaus in most large cities in the United States that will take a tape and return finished COM at a nominal price. COM is useful when large volumes of information that is unlikely to need changes, additions, or deletions and is not frequently accessed must be stored in retrievable form. In a pharmacy operation, COM might be used for profiles of inactive patients.

Digital to Analog Devices

Sometimes referred to as D/A converters, digital to analog devices interface computers to the real world by converting digital information into an equivalent voltage or current. This electrical output can be used in several ways, for example, to control a motor, to turn on or off lights, or to ring a bell. The plotters mentioned earlier use D/A converters to control motors attached to a pen by pulleys and strings. D/A converters are also useful in robotics, but, until robotics becomes important in pharmacy systems, pharmacists are unlikely to use D/A devices.

Voice and Music

Computers that can pronounce words as if they were spoken are not new. In reality, these are specialized analog output devices. Talking chessboards that issue challenges to a game of chess have been available in toy stores for years. Now, devices have been designed to allow computers to generate the spoken word under software control. It is tempting to imagine the day when users will instruct computers vocally and receive their answers vocally. The music synthesizers that enrich the lives of some are, in reality, computers in which the input device is an organ keyboard and the output device is a specialized analog output signal. The pocket translator that converts spoken word to spoken word seems not far off, but none of this has any particular application to pharmacy systems. Or does it?

COMMUNICATION DEVICES

Two-way exchange of information between a peripheral device (e.g., CRT) and a computer or between one computer and another is established by communication devices. For such processes to be successful, standards must be set, and these standards are very complex when they involve computers. Standards are necessary for the speed of transmission, number of transmission lines, voltage/frequency/time definitions of 1 and 0, and hand-shaking signals.

Speed must be standardized because there are very few communication channels that can handle information accurately as rapidly as a CPU can. The number of communication channels must be standardized because computers can communicate either a bit at a time or a byte at a time. If they communicate a bit at a time, they are said to be communicating in serial mode. If they communicate a byte at a time, they are in parallel communication. Voltage/frequency/time definitions of 1 and 0 are essential for clarity of communication. In some systems, a higher frequency could be defined as a 1 and a lower frequency as a 0, while the opposite could be true in others. Some systems use a direct current voltage instead of a frequency to signify a 1 or a 0. Hand-shaking signals determine which device will send, which will receive, and whether the sending and receiving devices are ready. They sometimes also include an acknowledgment that the data have been received.

Parallel Communication

Unfortunately, there are not widespread standards for parallel communication, probably because most parallel communication is performed over short distances. The cost of eight or more communication lines to be used simultaneously over long distances has been prohibitive. Most parallel communication occurs between a mainframe and a local printer, plotter, CRT, or other device, using custom designed parallel interface circuits. For a given bit rate (baud rate or number of bits sent and received per second), the parallel communication is at least N times faster than the serial device, where N is the number of channels used. In parallel devices, several additional channels are usually added to handle the hand-shaking signals. Parallel communication devices vary widely in price. Sometimes they are not available separate from the device interfaced.

Serial Communication

Serial data communication can be either synchronous or asynchronous. In both modes, the device is interfaced to the mainframe via an input/output (I/O) interface that attaches to the data bus. Standards vary for these serial I/O interfaces. Devices may be directly connected from I/O port to I/O port by means of one or more pieces of wire, or they may make use of telephone lines using a modulator/demodulator (modem) or an acoustic coupler. The modem converts digital signals to frequencies and vice versa (MOdulates and DEModulates). An acoustic coupler turns these electrical frequencies into audible sounds and converts audible sounds into electric frequencies. Usually, a modem is sold with a built-in acoustic coupler, since serial data communication usually takes place by telephone lines. Some special modems work without an acoustic coupler, generating electrical signals directly on the telephone line. These devices require special Federal Communications Commission (FCC) approval to be manufactured.

It is usually necessary to have serial communication in two directions. When this two-way communication occurs simultaneously, the system is said to be in full duplex. If the devices take turns communicating, then the system is said to be in half duplex. Most modems have a switch that enables them to communicate in either mode.

In synchronous communication, the transmitting device must continuously send valid data words at the specified speed. One character (hexadecimal 69) is defined as a synchronization (synch) character; it cannot be used to signify data. When the transmitting device has no data to send, it sends a stream of synch characters. The receiving device ignores synch characters in interpreting the data received. Synchronous communication devices are incompatible with asynchronous devices. Existing standards for synchronous serial data communication are, for the most part, proprietarily owned and used only in products from a single company.

Asynchronous serial communication is better standardized. In asynchronous communication, the transmitting device sends data only when it has some ready to send. Each data word is preceded by a single synchronization bit and followed by one or two stop bits. A parity bit that serves as a check on the integrity of the communication channel is usually placed between the data word and the stop bits. If the protocol is odd parity, then the number of on bits sent will be odd. If an even number of bits are received, it is evident that there is a breakdown in communications. The parity bit is made 1 or 0 in the data word before it is sent to ensure that the correct number of 1 bits are sent.

The universal standard for the start bit is 0. Five, six, seven, or eight data bits may follow, depending on the standard. One parity bit follows. The universal standard for one or two stop bits is that they are 1. Standard RS232 specifies a seven-bit data word with one start, one parity, and two stop bits. Most serial communication devices are available in RS232-compatible form. This standard also specifies standard connectors (DB-25) that allow interconnecting of compatible devices. It takes eleven bits in RS232 to send one character.

Common standard speeds available are 110 baud (10 characters per second or cps), 300 baud (27 cps, commonly rounded up to 30 cps), and 1,200 baud (commonly called 120 cps). At speeds of greater than 1,200 baud, standard, unconditioned telephone lines are usually unsuitable for data communication. Special "conditioned" lines may be leased from the telephone company, but they are expensive. The cost of an I/O interface varies significantly from mainframe to mainframe.

Chapter 4

Systems Development: A Cogent Approach

4

Millions of dollars are wasted annually by using computers to do nothing of particular value, and this does not include the use of computers for entertainment, which can be considered a constructive use. The reason for this waste is an insufficient development effort on the part of many designers. Most commonly, it results from ignorance of the proper procedures. Some of the blame must be taken by managements that have unreasonable expectations as to how fast a system can be implemented. Regardless of who is to blame, the result may be a system that does not meet any of the objectives set for it (rarely), a system that meets the wrong objectives (common), a system that meets the objectives inefficiently or cost-ineffectively (common), or a system that works well but alienates people who must use it, causing personnel problems (less common).

INTRODUCTION TO SYSTEMS

A system is "a series of actions which combine to achieve a goal." Characteristics of systems are that they use energy, require information, and go from states of lower to higher entropy. By this definition, nearly any activity (e.g., going to work in the morning) can be considered a system. As long as it uses actions to achieve a goal, it can be studied as a system.

Actions are the atomic elements of a system. The arrangement of these elements in an efficient sequence constitutes the core activity of systems design. Systems can be described in terms of people, procedures (actions), supplies, and equipment. Procedures relate the people to the actions that comprise the system. Supplies are passive and equipment is active under the control of people who perform according to the procedures.

The approach to systems development should take a life cycle (wholistic or heuristic) viewpoint. The first step in this approach is to propose to management that a systems analysis be performed. If this is approved, a team is formed, objectives are formulated, and the existing system is analyzed. Following this, similar systems from other organizations and those offered for sale are analyzed to determine whether they meet the objectives chosen. Then, an evaluation of the information gathered is written as a proposal either to design or to purchase a system. If a proposal to design a system is accepted, the system design phase is entered. If any proposal has been accepted, an implementation plan is prepared. The next steps are testing and implementation of the chosen system. The last step is an ongoing one, managing and controlling (modifying, if necessary) the system.

PROPOSAL TO PERFORM SYSTEMS ANALYSIS

The purpose of a proposal to perform systems analysis is to explain to management (1) why a systems analysis should be performed, (2) what resources it will require, (3) what the plans for proceeding are, and (4) what outcome is expected. An example of a proposal to perform systems analysis is included as Appendix E.

The problem definition should include the specific reason for the proposal, its estimated cost, and an outline of the remainder of the report. After this, it is usually best to proceed directly to the anticipated benefits, noting that some of the most important benefits involve risk reduction rather than active accomplishments.

The preliminary statement of performance requirements and constraints for the existing system is optional, but it is used by some analysts to indicate the scope of the system to be analyzed. It also documents the approach that will be used as a starting point for system design. In the first part of this section, the subsystems that comprise the system to be analyzed are identified. In the next part, the information required for each subsystem and its most likely source are indicated. The next part contains an analysis of the interdependency of the subsystems in terms of their information needs so that a decision on whether to analyze the whole system or just certain parts can be made with an understanding of the implications for the whole system. The final part of this section is a listing of absolute constraints upon any possible system design. Generally, these constraints can be identified without systems analysis.

The scope of the proposed analysis is presented in the next section. If the analysis will cover more than the existing system, the number and depth of other analyses to be performed should be identified.

The next section is a preliminary identification of the facts and sources that the team will need. In accepting the proposal, the administration gives its approval to the use of this information by the analysis team. In the next section, it is usually best to identify any foreseeable problems that are likely to affect the system.

The following section is an estimation of the personnel required to perform the analysis. If the team composition is in question, a breakdown by department and employee classification may be desired. The purpose of this proposal is only to give an estimate of the cost of the analysis, however, and such a breakdown may be too elaborate as well as premature. A final plan of analysis is produced only if the proposal is accepted. It is usually wise to estimate on the high side, since systems analyses tend to take 90 percent of the available time to do 10 percent of the work, leaving only 10 percent of the time to do the rest. The final section of the proposal is actually the table of contents of the report that management will receive if the analysis is approved.

The proposal to perform systems analysis is usually presented in person to hospital management, with copies available for review. At what stage to involve the hospital systems department is largely a matter of personal judgment. If the hospital has a well-staffed, progressive systems department, it is usually advantageous to involve them before the proposal is written. At other institutions, it may be best simply to invite them to the presentation of the proposal. If it is proposed that an existing computer system be replaced with a new one, the cooperation of the systems staff will be crucial to analyzing the existing system. If the hospital administration has already decided to implement a computerized pharmacy system and given full responsibility to the systems staff, it may be necessary to direct the proposal to this staff. Regardless of the order of progression of administrative events, it is very unwise to proceed with any design effort without first performing some degree of systems analysis. If necessary, pharmacy management should be adamant about this.

TEAM FORMATION

After an analysis effort has been approved, the next step may be to form a systems analysis team. In some cases, this will have already been done by management. This team will need two basic kinds of skills: systems and pharmacy. Occasionally, individuals with skills in both are available, and they usually belong on the team. If not, individuals from both departments must be on the team. Systems personnel usually feel that they should lead the team; however, hospital pharmacists know hospital pharmacy systems better than anybody else, and it is not unreasonable for a pharmacist to lead the analysis team. In many instances, a pharmacist is actually more efficient in this role, owing to an intimate knowledge of the system being analyzed. For instance, a pharmacist is likely to know if there is a policy and procedure manual, where it is kept, what shape it is in, and how certain procedures have been modified, ad hoc, by the staff. A systems department staff person as an "outsider," is unlikely ever to receive such candid information. Furthermore, a pharmacist-led team is less likely to have a negative effect on departmental morale. Regardless of who leads the team, the goal of the team is to produce an analysis document that accurately summarizes the operation of the system(s) under study.

The team's two basic tasks are to gather information about the system(s) in question and to assemble this information in a way that makes it easier to understand. Systems analysts have experience in gathering information about systems objectively. Many times, all data concerning the system(s) are gathered by systems staff. In many cases, however, pharmacists can provide information "off the top of their heads." This works well for qualitative information (e.g., procedures) but not usually at all for quantitative information (e.g., number of times a phone is used per hour). It is usually best if both systems personnel and pharmacists collect data. The pharmacists can ensure that systems staff draw the right conclusions about what they seem to see, and systems staff can provide objective feedback to pharmacists about the way in which the hospital pharmacy appears to work.

OBJECTIVES IDENTIFICATION

The first task of the analysis team is to identify the objectives of the system to be designed. A concise statement of what the system is supposed to do becomes essential when the system is being designed and trade-offs must be made. It also provides standards for subsequent evaluation. Besides, as the guru said, "If you don't know where you are going, you will probably wind up somewhere else."

Obviously, the analysis team cannot establish the objectives, but they must state clearly and concisely (and communicate) the objectives held by those who do set them. To do this, the team must interview those in authority over the system. Once the overriding principle or objective is thus set, others involved with the operation or management of the system can be invited to submit corollaries that represent wants or needs that the system could or should meet. All of these objectives are then organized by the analysis team according to what subsystem each affects. The unedited collection is then submitted to all levels of management for comment and approval, starting with the highest level and proceeding to the staff level. Substantive edits suggested are incorporated into a final draft, which then goes to the hospital administration for final approval.

At this stage, objectives should be written in the correct form. Well-written objectives express a concrete action that the system can perform and can be observed performing. Statements such as "The system shall be safe." are useless as objectives. A more useful objective states, "The system ensures patient safety by allowing pharmacist review of original physician orders." The rule of thumb here is: if it cannot be measured or observed, it does not exist. The overriding principle of what the system should do can always be stated in one sentence, sometimes referred to as the problem statement.

OPERATIONAL SYSTEM ANALYSIS

The word *analysis* is taken from the Greek word *analyein,* which means to break up. This is literally what the analysis of the existing system (operational system analysis) is intended to accomplish. The objective is to examine closely what and how many actions comprise the existing system. When this has been done, an attempt is made to describe the system simply and concisely on paper.

The methods used to gather information about the operational system vary as widely as the systems themselves vary. Usually, several methods are employed in a single analysis. One significant method is to interview people who work in the system and try to determine how the system works—without psychologically threatening those interviewed. The fact that people are often defensive about how they do what they do limits the usefulness of this technique in some instances. When this technique is used, the interviewer usually starts at higher levels of management and works down to the lowest level of staff. In conducting these interviews, the analyst usually has one open-ended session in which the employee (especially a managerial employee) is asked simply to explain how the system operates. This may be followed later by a second session in which the analyst directs questions about specific aspects of the system to the employee. The second session usually follows discussions with subordinate staff.

Another popular technique of systems analysis is forms analysis. When information is exchanged repeatedly between people who work together, there seems to be a human tendency to design a form so that people will not be required to write down the same information over and over. Systems analysts can make use of these forms. Employees are asked to submit copies of all forms used in their facilities. The information being transferred on these forms implies certain things about the system's operation. The analysts take a close look at each form and then draw conclusions (i.e., about what and how many actions are implied by the existence of this form). To avoid incorrect deductions in forms analysis, it is very important to exclude unused forms (i.e., "We're supposed to fill in that form but nobody does.") and to include every form that is used routinely (especially the hand-designed forms that the secretary makes with a photocopier).

Since procedures are statements of what the person does and what the person does almost always depends on the circumstances, procedures usually take the form of if . . . then. In many instances, the computer will be providing information to people about conditions on which they should take action. For this and other reasons, systems analysts sometimes use an information-tracing technique in which they identify all the types of information needed by people in order for the system to operate properly. This information is then traced through the system to determine every place that it affects an action of the system. Some analysts simultaneously do a subsystem and intersystem interface analysis. In this technique, the operational system is broken down into logical subsystems. Information flow into and out of each subsystem is then tabulated to determine the interdependency of the subsystems within the operational system. This determination is useful if less than the entire system is to be modified at one time. A similar analysis of information coming into and going out of the operational system as a whole is useful when procedures for gathering or distributing this information are to be modified, as they usually are. Forms analysis is sometimes used as a source for information-tracing techniques.

Once a fairly accurate picture of the actions and decisions that constitute the operational system has been obtained, quantitative information must be gathered. Most people seem to think of a systems analyst as a person holding a stopwatch while watching employees go about their jobs, but actual stopwatch-in-hand timing of tasks is not used very much anymore. To analyze a system properly, however, it is essential to have reliable, factual, quantitative information.

One popular technique is interrupt event counting. With this technique, employees are given a device that randomly sounds a beeper at 5- to 15-minute intervals and a card listing the activities that they usually perform. The employees are then instructed to stop whatever they are doing every time the device goes off and to check off whatever they were doing when the device sounded. Obviously, this slows the employees in their work. Since this affects the validity of the measurements, some analysts feel that an independent observer is needed. Even this is likely to impede the performance of some employees, however. In order for independent observers to be at all successful, the employees must be informed that they are not being evaluated, but rather, the system is being evaluated. A number of mathematical models are available to determine the number of events per unit of time and the time to perform each. A large enough sample of events must be counted to allow statistically correct deductions to be made about the workload of the operational system.

ALTERNATIVE SYSTEMS ANALYSES

Having obtained detailed information about the operational system, analysts must now examine the way other systems do the same thing. This may be done through on-site visits of local hospital pharmacies (sometimes done reciprocally) and through requests for proposals sent to vendors of hospital pharmacy computer systems.

Since on-site visits are usually performed in one or at most two days, they must take an abbreviated form; a quick, qualitative systems analysis must be performed. Only managerial and systems staff are interviewed. Facilities are toured, samples of forms are collected, and any existing analysis documentation is borrowed and photocopied. Each alternative system is compared with the operational system by means of parallel columns. Taking along a preliminary version of this document in which the columns allocated to the alternative systems are blank may help analysts to remember what questions to ask when performing the on-site review. It is important to visit a facility geographically as close to the operational system as possible. Regional differences in legislation and standards of care may have an impact on the value of the alternative system analysis to a design effort. Obviously, the more similar in size the two institutions are, the more useful the comparisons will be.

A request for proposal asks system vendors to supply an objective, qualitative, and quantitative analysis of the systems they sell. Such a request must make it clear that:

- The desire to obtain a new system is sincere. Usually, a copy of the operational systems analysis and objectives statement establish this point, as well as a few others.
- The vended system will not be considered unless all questions on the request for proposal are answered.
- The system will be tested against the statements made on any proposal received before it will receive final acceptance payment. The hospital's legal counsel can usually help in writing the document so that it makes this point.

The vendors are asked for a proposal to provide a system that meets the objectives as stated and can replace the operational system (i.e., can interface with the hospital in much the same way that the operational system does). Specific constraints and wanted or needed features are itemized, sometimes in the form of a series of questions (e.g., Does the proposed system provide for expiration dating of extemporaneously compounded injections?) Blank spaces are sometimes left after each question for vendors to enter their responses. When this is done, data are easier to compare later, and more vendors are likely to complete the request for proposal.

An alternative method is simply to state the desired features and constraints, indicating which are required and which are just wanted. In this instance, some vendors are likely to submit a standard general purpose proposal. In either approach, analysts should ask for the price of a system that meets all the constraints, has all the required features, and can handle the workload projected for the system over the next five years. An itemized price list for features that are wants should also be requested. The better vendors will also be able to provide system flowcharts, which are very useful in comparing systems.

Once the proposal deadline has been reached and the proposals collected, each system goes through a minianalysis, being compared, action for action, subsystem for subsystem, with the operational system. The analysis team must come to a decision at this point: whether to recommend a design effort or the acceptance of a proposal. This decision is presented to the hospital administration in the form of a systems analyses completion report (Appendix F). This report is often in narrative form, followed by extensive appendixes that provide details of the material summarized in the narrative. Basically, everything promised in the proposal to perform systems analyses is provided. The objectives statements are also resubmitted for reapproval at this time. The restatement of objectives is followed by a proposal either to contract for a particular vended system or to initiate a design effort. The format of this proposal includes (1) what is proposed; (2) briefly, why it is proposed; (3) how much it will cost; (4) a plan for proceeding; and (5) implications of nonacceptance of the proposal. Any differences between the operational system and the proposed system should be duly noted.

The systems analyses completion report is usually given to management in person. The entire analysis team should be present to answer any questions that arise.

SYSTEM DESIGN

If the proposal is to contract for a vended system, the design effort is minimal. The creation of an implementation plan may begin. If a design

Modularization

The best approach is to divide and conquer. In the analysis effort, the operational system was broken down into its composite actions. In the design effort, the actions are reassembled, along with new ones intended to accomplish new objectives. Usually, this is done in modules. The actions in a module are first drawn as a flowchart. Information required from inside or outside the computer system is specified, and procedures for gathering or inputting the information needed by the module are written. Outputs of the module are usually described by means of output layouts, which specify the information elements of the output and their format. An attempt is usually made to create a single limited number of information files, called master files, that are shared by modules throughout the system. Sometimes these files are defined first to eliminate redundancy errors and save costs associated with duplication of memory storage devices.

Master File Design

Master file design is probably the single most important step in system design. Fortunately, in the systems analysis effort, the information needs of the operational as well as alternative systems were determined, and these needs indicate the information also required in the system to be designed. Some of this information (e.g., drug name, strength, product size) is used many times daily and thus must be available on a fast random access device, such as a disk. Other information (e.g., address of drug manufacturer for direct ordering) is needed less often and may be stored on slower, sequential access devices, such as tape.

When the master files are designed, not only the effort necessary to gather the information, but also the maintenance required must be considered. Pharmacy-oriented data bases are available in computer-compatible media, most notably the Drug Products Information File (DPIF), published by the American Druggist Blue Book Data Center, Palo Alto, California, in association with the American Society of Hospital Pharmacists. Subscribing to such a data base service saves a significant amount of time and effort in collecting and maintaining master files. Since the layout of these files is fixed, it may be wise to use this layout directly when designing modules. Empty space is usually left in certain areas of these files to allow the insertion of information needed by a particular system design. Alternatively, it may be preferable to write a program that selectively extracts the information needed from such a file and puts it into the format chosen for a particular file. The desirability of flexibility in structuring an individual master file layout must be weighed against the continual cost of processing all records added to it.

SYSTEM CONTROLS

In addition to procedures for performing the work of the system, procedures are needed to control the system. Since much of the workload directly involves the computer system, much of the information needed for control is available in the computer. Other information may need to be collected and entered manually. Programs must be written and procedures devised to create reports needed by management to maintain control. These reports may be routinely produced (e.g., daily unit doses dispensed total) or produced by exception. In the latter case, a report is produced automatically only when a set of previously defined circumstances have been met (e.g., produce total unit doses dispensed report if there is greater than 10 percent variance between today and yesterday). The need for these reports can be anticipated via the objectives and analyses.

Additional routine and one-time reports will be increasingly requested as a progressive management staff becomes attuned to their value. Such reports can be used to support day-to-day and even long-range decisions. Since it is impossible to anticipate the format and constitution of every report that will eventually be needed, all significant data produced by the system must be preserved in a format that renders them usable for report generation.

Data base management systems (DBMS) are prewritten, wide-ranging programs that facilitate such data storage and retrieval. Report generators are programs that take data retrieved and put them into a user-defined format. Some DBMS have integral report generators; others are purchased separately. Sometimes an entire system is designed around DBMS, with all inputs, storage, and outputs being performed by DBMS interfaces to higher level languages. This works well in an environment where slack computer resources—additional work that an idle system could perform— are available. However, DBMS are designed to store any kind of information for any possible future use. They are inherently slower than specifically designed programs for input, storage, processing, and output, but specifically designed programs may render future use of data more difficult. Use of the master file concept in conjunction with specifically designed programs reduces the difficulty associated with future use, but does not

Systems Development

eliminate it entirely. Resolving the difficulties in creating efficient yet flexible DBMS remains a subject of research in computer science. For the present, it may be best to have flexible DBMS and report generator available that can load and manipulate files when needed, but not to rely too heavily on its use in daily processing.

BACKUP SYSTEM

Another system that must be designed, even though it may not appear on any of the operational system analysis charts, is the backup system. A backup system is a manual system that can be implemented when the computer fails. Every computer fails at least once during its life cycle, even if only at the end. The more complex parts a system is composed of, the greater the likelihood that it will fail within a given period of time. Several types of backup systems are used to handle this eventuality. One type of backup is the uninterruptible power supply, which is an electrical/electronic device that senses power failures and reacts to them so fast that little or no interruption of normal computer operation occurs during power failures. Chances are that a hospital's normal backup power system takes a second or two before it begins replacing power to all systems. This is generally long enough for a computer to forget almost everything it knows. Special rapid switching power supply devices are available in many sizes particularly for this application.

Redundant equipment and parallel processing are the most expensive but also the most effective backup to a computer system. The likelihood of all equipment failing at the same time is relatively low, assuming uninterruptible power supply systems have been implemented. This type of backup is used primarily when patient safety can be ensured only by continued operation of the equipment.

Another approach to backing up a system is to make arrangements to use a computer at another location via communications devices. This works best when there is another institution in the immediate geographical area with a computer of the same model that is slack a significant amount of the time. If another computer model is to be used as a backup, the programming effort in developing the backup system can be significant. Also, the maintenance of backup programs can be difficult, if not impossible.

By far the easiest, least costly, and most commonly used type of backup system is the manual backup system. In this type of backup, when the computer goes down, all information that would have been input into the computer is written or typed onto forms. Sometimes mark sense forms, which allow rapid entry of data after computer recovery, are used. All material that would have been output by the computer is typed or written on the same forms that the computer printer would have used. Procedures must be written for staff to perform any information processing that the computer would ordinarily perform. However, only those processes essential for patient safety must be performed.

Obviously, implementation of any backup system requires additional personnel. Procedures for obtaining these personnel should be created. Recovery procedures must also be written. One very important set of recovery procedures involves updating files to reflect activity during system downtime and checking for file damage caused by the system going down. The main system should be designed to provide backup copies of all master files on a periodic (usually daily) basis. Then, if a file should be destroyed, a relatively current copy of that file is available. If all additions and deletions made on that file since the backup copy was made can be determined, the current file can be reconstructed from the backup copy. This is not always possible, however. Because loss of a file can affect patient safety, most systems maintain a redundant backup on daily transactions. Sometimes carbon copies of all labels printed are kept for a week or so in case a file is lost. Other systems save original physician order forms for the same reason. Companies with which hospitals contract for hardware repair services must have an implicit understanding of the urgent nature of the need for repair. Once the normal backup systems have been designed, they must be tested before they can possibly be implemented.

HUMAN FACTORS

Aside from ensuring that all objectives are met, the system design process must take into account many human factors. Placement of noisy equipment is one aspect of this. It should also be remembered that humans do not always like to be beeped at. Most computers are capable of disarming or changing the frequency and pitch of audible signal devices. Voice output modules might improve morale of the staff. Legibility of output that humans are required to read is also important to morale. There is little more frustrating than having to peer at a computer-printed document or cathode ray terminal screen in order to figure out what it says, especially when in a hurry. Aesthetic appearance of computer equipment probably affects human performance more than is commonly recognized. Furthermore, humans expect a computer to acknowledge correct entry of data. If it is not possible for the machine to repeat the information received, it should at least give a signal (e.g., beep, buzz, click) that valid information has been received.

One human factor that is difficult to combat is monotony. Some jobs related to computers (e.g., data entry) will probably always be monotonous. This may be combatted by assigning a variety of entry tasks to data entry operators or by allowing the operators to vary the equipment used at will. For example, keyboard, light pen, and touch screen entry equipment might be provided with options in the program for using any of the three. These human aspects should not be dismissed as extras. Downtime, sick time, and high staff turnover resulting in hiring and training expense are examples of when poor planning for the human factor costs real dollars.

Implementation Plan

Once the design is complete, an implementation plan must be formulated. The major steps are writing programs, obtaining equipment, writing procedures in a form for use by employees, and obtaining supplies. In communicating this plan, it is sometimes useful to utilize a graphic method, such as the program evaluation and review technique (PERT) chart.

Following this, the system design report and implementation plan are presented to the hospital administration as a proposal. The objectives of the system are submitted for final reapproval at this step. Cost estimates and specifications for personnel, hardware, supplies, and equipment are also a part of this report, and these will be used in the next step—soliciting proposals from vendors and hiring new staff.

TESTING AND IMPLEMENTATION

Assuming a design or purchase proposal has been approved, the system must now be built, tested, and implemented. Equipment and supply requests for proposals are submitted to potential vendors with detailed specifications. When proposals have been received, they are evaluated and a selection is made. Programmers are brought in to write programs based on flowcharts created in the design phase. Department staff are oriented and educated in the tasks they will perform in the new system. Staff outside the department are informed of changes in interdepartment information exchange and are oriented to any new procedures that affect them. It is very important that all levels of management and staff clearly understand the operation of the new system. Employees should be encouraged to put forward candidly any problems they foresee with the system. When programs have been written and equipment obtained, the programs are tested and debugged (the errors are corrected). All bench testing is completed and the system installed. Parallel testing is performed and, if results are satisfactory, the system is allowed to operate.

For the sake of future reference, a report of events that occur during implementation should be written. Data gathered to ensure that the system is working, data to document cost-effectiveness of the system, workload data to back up projections during analysis, and final operational and start-up cost projections are among the items to be included on this report.

Usually, a set of testing procedures for both normal and backup systems is designed as part of the design effort. These procedures may require test programs. The system constraints identified earlier may serve as a guideline in testing. Most of the test procedures need to be performed only once to reveal flaws in design and programming. Some of the test procedures may be useful in checking system integrity after system downtime. All of these procedures must be fully documented in a manner that would allow new personnel to understand how to perform them.

Testing usually has three phases: initial bench testing, installed testing, and postrecovery testing. In the initial bench testing, data are fed to the programs and the resulting output is compared with expected output. It is important to do bench testing with both valid (i.e., correct format and range) and invalid data, since invalid data, processed correctly, can cause serious problems. Installed testing is performed only after bench testing shows the system to be working. The system is installed in its final configuration, and the people who will actually work with the system give it a test. Quite often this is done in parallel with the old manual system. It is assumed that satisfactory performance in normal operation is the truest test of the system, but it usually takes about a year for the system to get a "worst case test under fire" in this scheme. Therefore, it is usually a good idea, in addition to a parallel test, to devise an in situ worst case test for the system to determine if the system can handle it. Postrecovery testing involves a set of procedures to be performed before the system is used again after it has been down for one reason or another. Many of these can be minor modifications of procedures developed for bench and installed testing phases. This type of testing should be a short (less than one hour) series of tests that can be performed to ensure as far as possible that nothing (i.e., programs, data, or equipment) was damaged by whatever caused the system to go down.

Chapter 5

A Hypothetical Pharmacy System

5

By reviewing the design and operation, nuts and bolts style, of a hypothetical unit dose hospital centralized pharmacy computer system, it is possible to (1) examine the basic parts of a typical system, (2) show what a comprehensive system might do, and (3) stimulate industry or practitioners to provide better pharmacy services by using computers. The approach used here is unusual, so a few words of explanation are in order. Pascal-like data structure descriptions for the "standard" system are presented first. These consist of true Pascal variable, constant, and type declarations followed by prose descriptions of the meanings or significance of the structures where necessary. A series of Pascal-like procedures and functions is presented next consisting of true Pascal procedure or function headers, identifying variable names and types, followed by prose descriptions of what the procedure or function actually does. Although the actual Pascal statements necessary to accomplish this have been omitted, the main algorithm for the "program" has been included in the form of true Pascal control constructs interspersed with liberal amounts of prose explanation.

Thus, this whole chapter is a well-documented Pascal program without the fine details. If the sham procedures were filled in with real ones and the constructs modified to suit individual needs, the result would be a relatively complete hospital pharmacy computer system.*

---

* Material in this chapter is © 1983 by Aspen Systems. For further information, contact Permission Editor, Aspen Systems, Rockville, Md.

DATA STRUCTURES

In this program, extensive use is made of a data structure that can be described as a "dynamic binary tree of records." Pascal allows for dynamic data structures by using a special data type called pointer, signified by the ↑. The pointer data type can never be printed or saved on a mass storage file. Because it is the address of the data it points to, it is analogous to the ordinal position number used to identify a single data item in an array. A dynamic data structure differs from an array in that (1) the pointer cannot be calculated as an array ordinal can and (2) it is not necessary to determine ahead of time how many data items will go into the dynamic data structure as it is with an array.

The "binary tree" portion of the structure definition refers to a structure like that created in Appendix D. A binary tree is a data structure in which each record contains a pointer to one item with an alphabetically or numerically greater value and a pointer to one item with a similarly lesser value. For example, to create a binary tree for a formulary containing five drugs (aspirin, phenacetin, caffeine, acetaminophen, and codeine), we would take the first item as the root and draw it like this:

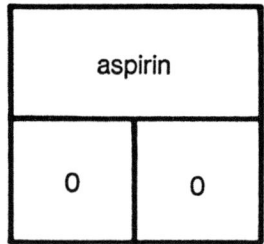

The boxes below aspirin are for the array ordinals of one data item alphabetically greater than and one data item alphabetically less than the word *aspirin*. The usual convention is that the left box (left pointer) is for less than and the right box is for greater than.

The array of the tree always keeps this assignment:

1. aspirin
2. phenacetin
3. caffeine
4. acetaminophen
5. codeine

An array has been used here simply to make the illustration clearer. In the actual structures, the ordinals shown as 1 through 5 would exist only

A Hypothetical Pharmacy System 107

as pointers. The items are never moved from these positions. The tree simply maintains pointers to their locations. The 1 through 5 can be thought of as array ordinals, pointers (memory addresses), or any other specification of the physical storage location of the data.

The next step in creating the tree is to compare the second data item with the root data item. Phenacetin has a value greater than that of aspirin, so 2 is placed into the right pointer for aspirin. The result is drawn like this:

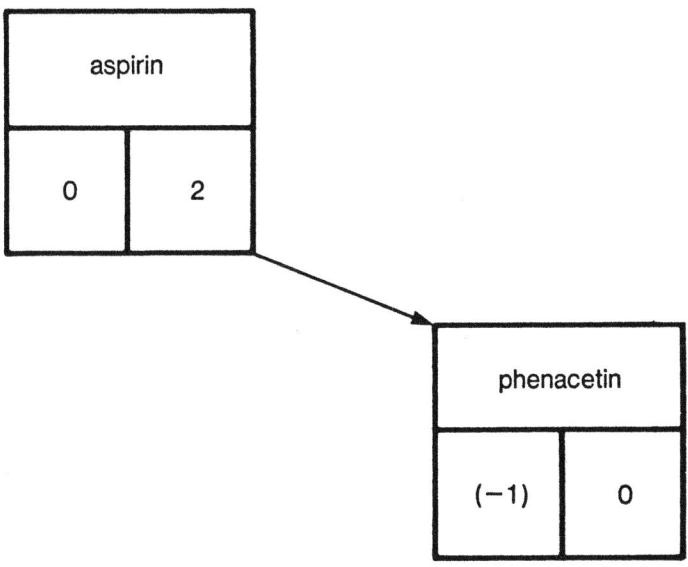

Some binary trees are double linked by indicating backward moves with negative pointers. In this example, phenacetin's left pointer points back to 1, a lesser alphabetic value. If the value of aspirin were greater, the negative pointer would be placed on the right. The 0 indicates that the tree has no entry with a value greater than that of phenacetin or less than that of aspirin.

The next step is to compare the third item with the root. Caffeine has a value greater than that of aspirin. Next the third entry is compared with the item pointed to by the right (greater than) pointer of the first item.

Because the alphabetic value of caffeine is less than that of phenacetin, phenacetin is given a left pointer to caffeine. This can be drawn thus:

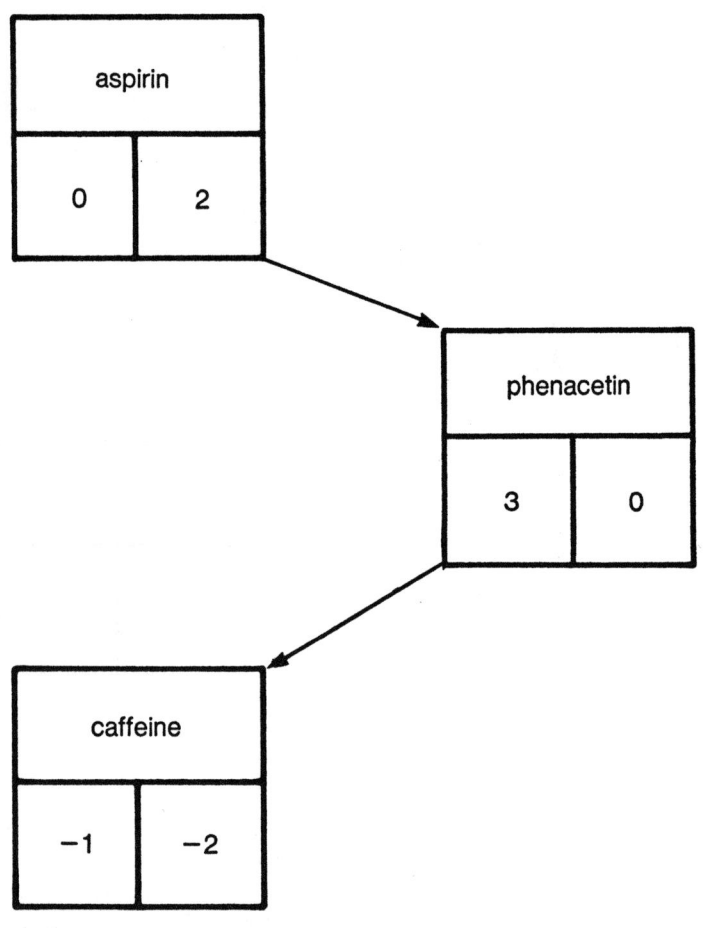

Next the fourth entry is compared with the root. The alphabetic value of acetaminophen is less than that of aspirin. Aspirin, the root, is given a left pointer. This is drawn thus:

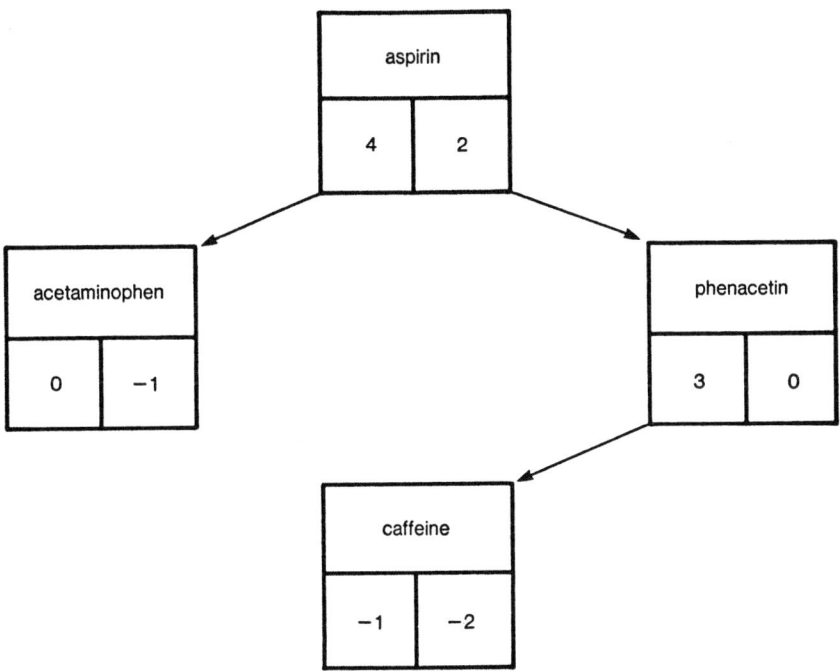

The negative pointer in acetaminophen points backward to a greater item.

The final step for this list is to compare the fifth entry with the root. Codeine has an alphabetic value greater than that of aspirin, so it is moved to the right. Codeine's value is less than that of phenacetin, so it is moved to the left. Codeine is greater than caffeine, so it is moved to the right.

Caffeine is given a pointer to codeine. Thus, the final tree would be drawn thus:

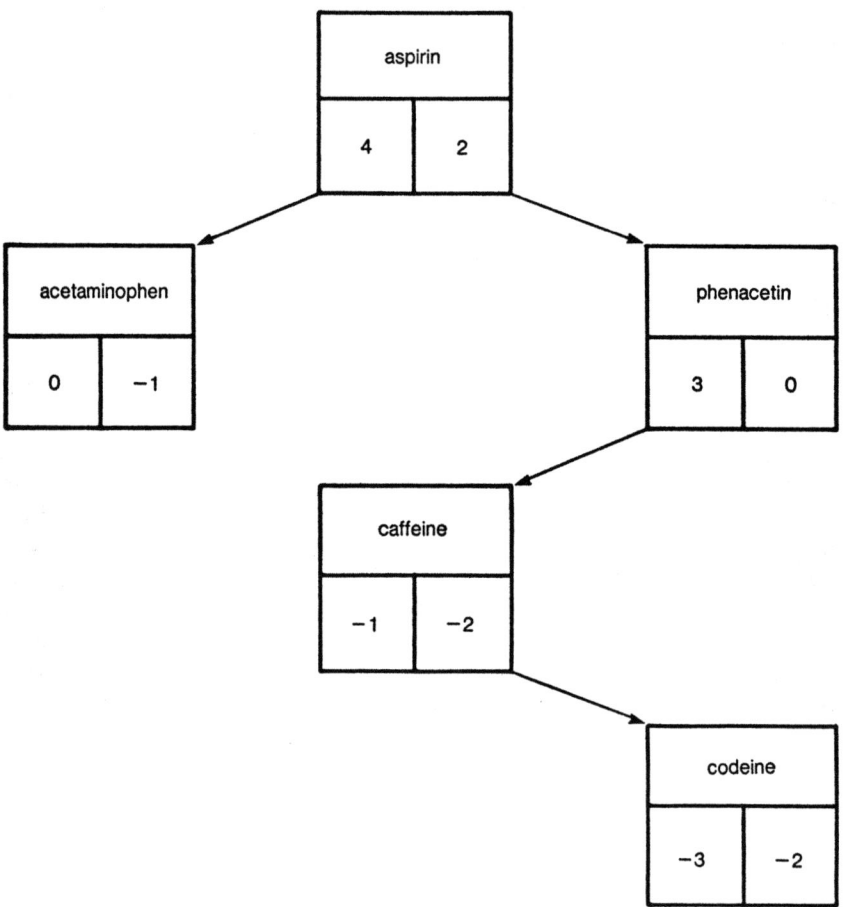

It is advantageous to use binary trees for several reasons. Adding new data to a binary tree does not require a complete resorting of the file. The data are placed at the bottom of the array and the pointers are calculated by comparison. Searching in binary trees is extremely fast, since each comparison eliminates half of the possible data items. Use of binary trees usually decreases the time spent reshuffling the arrays, because the array is left in order and the pointers are calculated. One major problem with binary trees is that the deletion of data is not a trivial process. Some programmers give up trying to delete data from binary trees in any elegant manner and simply reconstruct the tree from scratch, omitting the data to be deleted. This deletion approach works for smaller files, but other techniques must be used for larger files.

The data structures presented in the following are not designed to fit any particular hardware or software configuration. The presence of very large (>1 megabyte) primary memory, plus a very large, fast (>200 megabyte) disk storage device is assumed. Backup is assumed to be on magnetic tape. Case structure variant record types are presented in logical order, although this is incorrect syntactically. To be correct, all case variants would have to be grouped together at the end of the record and nested within a single variant.

The Patient Record

The file of patient records contains all the information specific to the patients served by the pharmacy. It is implemented in this example in Exhibit 5–1 as a binary tree of (long) records. The major subsections of it are name and address data, billing information, standing prescription orders, and clinical information. In this hospital pharmacy model, address data translates to room number. Since this changes every time a patient is admitted, discharged, or transferred, these data are sometimes referred to as admissions, discharge, and transfer (ADT) data. Many times a hospital already has a computerized ADT system that can send this information directly to the pharmacy system. Sometimes the pharmacy receives a printout with a list of all changes, which must then be entered immediately into the system. This part of the structure is pretty much the same in satellite, traditional, and unit dose hospital pharmacy systems. In an outpatient pharmacy system, these data are replaced by street, city, and zip code. Lack of a "captive audience" in the community pharmacy creates the need for a trade-off between the number of active records and the amount of mass memory in the system. Hospitals that are part of a group can take advantage of centralized mass storage to alleviate this problem. A patient may become inactive in one hospital, only to become active in another. Nothing is lost if all hospitals have equal access to the files. Of course, the old adage "garbage in, garbage out" applies here. If address records are not scrutinized and updated regularly, they become useless or even detrimental.

The next portion of the patient information file is billing information. In this example, billing information consists solely of an account number. In a typical hospital, this single 10- to 15-digit integer is sufficient to link pharmacy charges with the overall hospital accounting system. A truly wide variety of means can be used to submit patient charges to accounting

Exhibit 5–1 Patient Information Data Structure

Type		
cmpd	:	boolean;
std	:	boolean;
compliance	:	boolean;
patientptr	=	^patient;
drugptr	=	^rx;
allergyptr	=	^allergy;
problemptr	=	^problem;
noteptr	=	^note;
labptr	=	^labtest;
ingredientptr	=	^ingredient;
timeptr	=	^admintime;
doseptr	=	^missedose;
notelineptr	=	^noteline;
Patient	=	record
left patient	:	patientptr;
right patient	:	patientptr;
lastname	:	string;
firstname	:	string;
middlename	:	string;
roomnumber	:	string;
accountnumber	:	integer;
rxbase	:	drugptr;
allergybase	:	allergyptr;
problembase	:	problemptr;
notebase	:	noteptr;
labbase	:	labptr
end; {patient}		
Rx	=	record
rightrx	:	drugptr;
leftrx	:	drugptr;
genericnumber	:	0.99999999;
case compounded	:	boolean of
true	:	(ingredientbase : ingredientptr);
false	:	( );
routeofadministration	:	string;
numberofdosageforms	:	string;
case		
standardadministrationtime	:	boolean of
true	:	(key:0..99);
false	:	(admintimeptr : timeptr);
technician	:	string;
pharmacist	:	string;
physician	:	string;
firstdose	:	integer;
lastdose	:	integer;

Exhibit 5–1 continued

```
Rx (cont'd)
    case missedose              :   boolean of
        true                    :   ( );
        false                   :   (missedbase : doseptr)
end; {Rx}

Ingredient                      =   record
    rightingredient             :   ingredientptr;
    leftingredient              :   ingredientptr;
    name                        :   string;
    strength                    :   real;
    units                       :   string;
    quantity                    :   real;
    quantityunits               :   string;
    instruction                 :   string
end; {ingredient}

Admintime                       =   record
    righttime                   :   timeptr;
    lefttime                    :   timeptr;
    timeadmin                   :   0..2400
end; {admintime}

Missedose                       =   record
    rightdose                   :   doseptr;
    leftdose                    :   doseptr;
    timemissed                  :   0..2400
end; {missedose}

Allergy                         =   record
    rightallergy                :   allergyptr;
    leftallergy                 :   allergyptr;
    drugname                    :   string;
    allergygroup                :   integer;
    comment                     :   string
end; {allergy}

Problem                         =   record
    rightproblem                :   problemptr;
    leftproblem                 :   problemptr;
    prob                        :   string;
    SP                          :   boolean;
    startdate                   :   0..991231;
    stopdate                    :   0..991231
end; {problem}
```

Exhibit 5-1 continued

Note	=	record
rightnote	:	noteptr;
leftnote	:	noteptr;
notedate	:	0..991231;
line	:	notelineptr;
profession	:	(nurse, pharmacist, dietitian, physicaltherapist, physician, other)
notewriter	:	string
end; {note}		
Noteline	=	record
linenote	:	string;
nextline	:	notelineptr
end; {noteline}		
Labtest	=	record
righttest	:	labptr;
lefttest	:	labptr;
testname	:	string;
date	:	820101..991231;
time	:	0..2400;
result	:	real;
units	:	string;
comment	:	string
end; {labtest}		

systems, such as magnetic tapes, communications links (networks), optical character recognition, and keyboarding from printouts.

    The third part of the patient information file is composed of standing patient drug orders. This section repeats once for every current drug order. The complete identification of the drug and dosage form is defined by the first entry, the generic *number*. This is essentially a pointer to the formulary file, in which each generic number indicates a unique drug, dose, and dosage form. If the dosage form is one to be compounded by the pharmacy, the Pascal dynamic data structure shown in the example stores the formulation. Also included in the patient information file is the route of administration. In this example, a variable length alphanumeric string of up to 255 characters may be used. This allows greater flexibility, but it increases memory requirements, slows input operations, and makes it more difficult to format an output. In practice, these difficulties can be minimized by not entering any administration route unless it varies from that obviously indicated by the dosage form (e.g., rectal for rectal suppository, oral for tablets, sublingual for sublingual tablets).

The next datum is the number of dosage forms to be administered. The dosage to be given the patient can be determined by looking up the associated generic number in the formulary file and multiplying it by this number. The administration schedule key occupies the next field. This identifier indicates whether a standard administration schedule is to be followed or whether there is a special schedule. If there is a special schedule, the Pascal dynamic record structure shown in the example is used to store the administration times.

The next fields specify the physician writing the order, the technician recording it, or the pharmacist validating the order. In this example, these are shown as full character strings, but data could easily be compressed by using pointers to files containing the complete name of the person involved. Passwords could be used to provide additional security to the system.

The date and time of the first and last doses are placed in the next two fields. The next records, consisting of the date and time at which each unused dosage form was returned from the nursing station, repeat within each current order. It is assumed that all others were administered to the patient. If serial lot identification is to be used, this record must contain a reference to the serial lot number so that the correct status of the serial group may be maintained.

In a multidose, traditional hospital pharmacy system, this data structure is sufficient, except that the number of doses administered would be indeterminable (unless careful counts of vials returned are made and nursing staff have been persuaded not to tamper with the unused contents of vials). A typical system records each refill sent and the quantity in each.

The clinical information section of this example patient information file may seem rather idealistic, but, given the rapid decrease in the cost of mass storage devices, the development of more capable computers, and the advances being made in computer networking, such structures are quite realistic, especially in light of the pharmacist's increasingly clinical role in the hospital. In this example, these data structures are dealt with as though the data actually reside in the pharmacy's mass memory. In practice, with advanced networking systems, such data could be physically resident on any one of several host computers connected to the network (e.g., the laboratory's computer, the medical records department's computer).

The first segment of the patient clinical information substructure is the drug allergy history. As shown, this contains one short field for each drug to which the patient has shown an allergy and another field of up to 255 characters in which the reaction is described. A key to other potentially cross-reacting drugs is referenced back to the drug information file. This segment may be repeated for each drug to which the patient has had an allergic reaction.

The problem list repeats for as many problems as a health care practitioner feels should be included in the list. Each problem may be designated as status/post (SP) by setting the Boolean value of the SP variable to true. Each problem is described by a string of up to 255 characters. A start and stop date are included for each. The segment provided for the health care practitioner's progress notes concerning the patient's condition includes a place for the date, the note—as many lines as desired—the name of the practitioner, and the practitioner's professional role. This structure repeats as necessary.

The last segment of the clinical information structure is the laboratory report structure. For each laboratory test performed on the patient, the file provides room for the name of the test, the real numeric result, and the units used. Date and time are likewise included. A reduction in memory use at the cost of central processor time (the classic trade-off) is again possible by the use of pointers and a table for laboratory test names.

There is no reason for a difference between the clinical information portion of the structure in a multidose hospital pharmacy system and that of a unit dose hospital pharmacy system. The patient data are the same.

Formulary Data Structure

As shown in Exhibit 5-2, the formulary data structure is much more straightforward than the previous structure. Likewise, its purpose is more limited. This structure, again a binary tree of records, serves as a master reference list of drugs approved by the Pharmacy and Therapeutics (P&T) Committee and stocked by the pharmacy. The generic number is the unique identifier that specifies the drug, dose, dosage form, and supplier. In a way, it functions much like a pointer to the formulary file. Other data structures use the information in this file by storing the generic number. For human interaction, however, the integer value may be printed out and reviewed.

The strength field represents the real number of dose units in a single dosage form (for example, a codeine 30 mg tablet has strength equal to 30). The dose unit description represents the units of measure that correspond to the strength data. It may not include volume, since the strength is always the total dosage per dosage form. It is important to make this clear in defining the structure. The dosage form is a free format string. Although an enumerated data type (like the profession field of the note record shown in Exhibit 5-1) may be used for dosage form and dose unit, this would restrict the data to a limited set of valid entries. However, it

Exhibit 5-2 Formulary Data Structure

```
Type
   rxptr                       =  ^drug;
   supplierptr                 =  ^supplier;
   Drug                        =  record
      leftname                 :  rxptr;
      rightname                :  rxptr;
      genericname              :  string;
      genericnumber            :  0..99999999;
      strength                 :  real;
      doseunits                :  string;
      dosageform               :  string;
      supplier                 :  supplierptr;
      injectionvolume          :  0..2999;
      legendstatus             :  (OTC, Rx, CII, CIII, CIV, CV);
      acceptedPT               :  boolean;
      NDCcode                  :  0..9999999999;
      case charged             :  boolean of
         true                  :  (cost : real);
         false                 :  ( );
      case combination         :  boolean of
         true                  :  (otherdrug : rxptr);
         false                 :  ( )
   end; {drug}
```

would allow the record structure to be varied, storing appropriate additional information based on the type of dosage form.

The supplier identifier is actually a pointer to the supplier file. This information is useful in inventory control applications. Legend status is an enumerated data set that makes it possible to keep track of the legal status of items in stock and on the formulary. In this data structure model, no other distinction is made about the handling of controlled substances, since a perpetual inventory of all drugs in the hospital is assumed by the overall structure. Additional physical counts are made on controlled substances, but the data remain the same. Injection volume, which is included to allow the data structure to handle injections (it is 0 in noninjectable dosage forms), is the total volume of the dosage form, always in ml. For example, a 1 mg/ml injection in a 5-ml vial would be recorded as follows:

```
strength         : 5
doseunits        : mg
dosageform       : Inj vial
supplier         : not printable, since type is pointer
injectionvolume  : 5
```

The accepted PT entry is provided so that items not currently or not yet accepted by the P&T Committee can be put into the formulary. This might facilitate order flow in anticipation of P&T Committee approval. ND code is the National Drug Code assigned to the dosage form. Since it does not uniquely describe a drug and dosage form, it has no function in the data structure; it is included to facilitate billing of third party payers.

The next section of the data structure involves cost. Typically, some items are so low in cost that the pharmacy does not charge for them. If the charged status is false, no cost is kept in the file. Price to the patient for charged items is calculated by an algorithm decided on by the pharmacy or hospital administration. Using this method rather than storing the price facilitates changes in prescription pricing.

The last field is also a dynamic substructure. If the item is a combination drug, it is given one formulary entry with the generic number for the fixed combination; the dynamic structure in this field contains a pointer to the formulary entry for the first ingredient of the combination. The ingredients of combination records have the same structure as do regular formulary items, but they are pointed to via the pointer that is stored in the combination record definition. The left pointer is always nil. The next ingredient of the combination is indicated in order from the highest to lowest clinical significance through the right pointer field. When a nil right pointer is found in a series of ingredients to a combination, the last, least important ingredient has been found.

Inventory Data Structure

The data structure for inventory (Exhibit 5–3) is a binary tree of records with a slight twist. Instead of being ordered by one data element, the generic number, it is ordered by two elements, the generic number and

Exhibit 5–3 Inventory Data Structure

```
Type
    stockptr         =  ^ stocklevel;
    Stocklevel       =  record
        leftlevel        : stockptr;
        rightlevel       : stockptr;
        costcenter       : string;
        genericnumber    : 0..99999999;
        quantity         : 0..999999;
        userate          : real;
        ERP              : real;
        EOQ              : real;
    end; {stocklevel}
```

the cost center. This is done so that inventories may be easily listed in order by generic number within each cost center. The cost centers can be defined as desired for a particular system. Basically, a cost center is any separately administered group that can give or take formulary items.

In a satellite unit dose operation, typical cost centers are the central storage area and each satellite pharmacy. If controlled substances are kept in a drug room on each nursing station, each drug room may be considered a cost center. If each cost center is to be maintained on perpetual inventory, the system must be notified each time an item is added or removed from its stock. Maintaining perpetual inventories of each cost center not only reduces pilferage, but also, facilitates restocking because accurate figures on usage and current stock levels are always available. A cost center can also be an enumerated data type.

The generic number identifies which drug and dosage form is being kept in the record. Userate is the average rate of use, in dose units per day, for the cost center in question. This is calculated on a periodic basis, over a limited number of days, so that it always reflects the current status of usage of the item in that cost center.

The ERP is the economic reorder point, that is, the stock level at which it becomes economical for the cost center to reorder a supply of the item in question. This is generally most useful in regard to the total quantity in stock in the central drug storage area. If careful attention is paid to the holding cost and ordering cost for each cost center, however, it can be determined at what point the cost center needs to be restocked with the item.

The EOQ, economic order quantity, is closely related to the ERP. The EOQ is the quantity that should be ordered when an order is placed. It is calculated to minimize the dollars invested in drug inventory and the cost of placing orders. It is possible to calculate EOQs based on the probability of a stockout, as determined by a given usage rate. Conceivably, the probability of a stockout could be set for each item in a formulary based on the clinical significance of a stockout. In practice, any gains made by such fine tuning would probably be offset by losses as a result of fluctuating demands for drugs in the hospital pharmacy.

Serial Group Data Structure

By careful control of serial group data, every dosage form in the hospital can be accounted for from the day it arrives from the supplier to the day it is destroyed or given to a patient. The serial group data structure is shown in Exhibit 5-4. Basically, whenever stock is received by the pharmacy, each lot of a given generic number is divided into several serial

Exhibit 5-4 Serial Group Data Structure

```
Type
   groupptr              =    ^ serialgroup;
   Serialgroup           =    record
      leftgroup          :    groupptr;
      rightgroup         :    groupptr;
      serialno           :    0..99999999;
      genericnumber      :    0..99999999;
      costcenter         :    string;
      quantity           :    0..9999;
      expiredate         :    820101..991231;
      mfrlotno           :    string;
      orderno            :    0..99999999;
      datereceived       :    820101..991231
   end; {serialgroup}
```

groups, and each serial group is assigned a number. All items in a serial group should have the same manufacturer lot number and expiration date. The size of a serial group is determined by a few simple criteria. It should be small enough that an entire group can be economically transferred from one cost center to another. Thus, it should be smaller than the approximate size of the average EOQ of the smallest cost center using the item. It should be as large as possible within these guidelines, however, to minimize the personnel overhead associated with handling the groups. Many times, the manufacturer packages containers in groups that conveniently match the hospital's serial group size for the item. A data item that defines the serial lot size for each generic number can be added to the formulary.

Serial groups are banded or boxed together at the time the order is received and labeled with their serial group number. If desired, the serial group label can be printed on a graphics printer and can include optical bar code or some other pattern that can be recognized by a mechanical reader. This makes transaction processing much less expensive, since little or no personnel time (keyboarding) is necessary to enter transactions.

In the data structure shown in Exhibit 5-4, items can be grouped by manufacturer lot number at the time of order receipt. Efficient procedures to minimize personnel time spent setting up serial lots can be developed. This is an instance in which the pharmacist can use the computer to provide a type of service that has not been offered before, that is, complete assurance of recall and location of expired drugs.

Transaction Data Structure

The transaction file serves two basic purposes. It is a backup file for use in the event data are lost from a system disk, and it is a structure to contain data that modify other structures (i.e., transactions). The backup file is kept on magnetic tape and updated on a regular, periodic basis. New data are written over old data on a series of tapes, which are rotated in such a fashion that, at any given time, two fairly complete sets of data are available. Also, whenever a transaction is entered (typed on a keyboard or read by a mechanical device) the corresponding data bases are adjusted accordingly. The transaction is then written onto the tape and "forgotten" by the system. When the system fails, the data structure is recreated by loading the most recent master copy of the entire data structure, posting the most recent transaction tape to it, and then posting all transactions that occurred while the system was down (usually hand-written on forms).

The data structure shown in Exhibit 5-5 uses dynamic records to store three different kinds of transactions. Each transaction has in common a date and a time, which makes it possible to trace the status of the system back to any given time and date as needed. The patientout record variant is basically a repeat of the information contained in the patient record drug administration section. The difference is that, in the patient record drug administration section, information was recorded by exception and here each transaction is explicitly recorded. Thus, in a unit dose system, each time the patient medication drawers are checked and the returned items are entered, the system adjusts the stock levels and generates a transaction for each missing dose of a generic number. There is no serial number in

Exhibit 5-5 Transaction Data Structure

```
Type
  Kind                =   (patientout, costctr, supplierin);
  Trans               =   record
    date              :   820101..991231;
    time              :   0..2400;
    casekindof
      patientout      :   (genericnumber     :0..99999999,
                           accountnumber     :integer,
                           quantity          :0..9,
                           costcenter        :string);
      costcenter      :   (centerin          :string,
                           centerout         :string,
                           genericnumber     :0..99999999,
                           serialnumber      :integer);
      supplierin      :   (suppliernumber    :0..9999,
                           ordernumber       :0..9999999999,
                           itemnumber        :0..99,
                           quantity          :0..999999);
  end; {trans}
  Transactions        =   file of trans;
```

the patientout transaction because, within most existing systems, it would be impractical to label each dosage form with its serial number.

With the data structure presented in Exhibit 5-5, a serial group that has been transferred to a station is assumed to be rotated out on a first-in-first-out basis. This obviously hinders recall and expiration date checking. The only alternatives seem to be to omit the checking process altogether or to use an optical recognition schema, perhaps by enclosing each dosage form in some sort of envelope or jacket. The latter choice provides absolute expiration date and lot recall control with minimal personnel involvement. However, there are obvious costs associated with the envelopes and the personnel to fill them.

The first field of the patient-out type record is the generic number of the item, which identifies the item in the formulary that was given to the patient. The next item, the account number, identifies the patient. The quantity field is the number of dosage units. The cost center is the cost center that gave the item to the patient.

The transaction from one cost center to another may be visualized as the main pharmacy transferring stock to a satellite pharmacy. Centerin is a string variable that identifies the cost center receiving the stock; centerout, the cost center giving out the stock. Strings are used in the example to provide flexibility. The use of enumerated data types for centerin and centerout would have the possibly desirable effect of limiting certain cost centers to certain types of intercenter transactions. For example, if a type was defined as

```
        Type
            outcenters        : (mainpharmacy);
```

and centerout was defined as

```
            casekindof
                center        : (centerout:outcenters);
```

the Pascal compiler would write code that would trap any attempt to post a transaction that transferred stock from any cost center other than the main pharmacy. Whether this is desirable is ultimately up to the system manager—the pharmacy administrator—but the enumerated data types provided in Pascal do allow trapping of improper data. This kind of feature should be used whenever it is available in the language used to write a pharmacy system.

Only one serial group is included in the data structure (Exhibit 5-5). This does not preclude the algorithm from facilitating transfer of a block of sequential serial groups from one center to another, however. A routine that does this could easily be written.

The final transaction type shown in Exhibit 5-5 is the supplierin transaction. There is no cost center in this structure because this substructure records stock received from suppliers and it is assumed that there is only one cost center that is authorized to receive stock from outside the organization. If this is not the case, this structure would need a cost center data item. The supplier number refers to a file that contains information about each supplier with which the pharmacy does business. The order number and item number also refer to a file. The order number is the specific purchase order sent to the supplier by the pharmacy; the item number is a specific item on that order. The quantity of dosage units received may differ from the quantity ordered because of supplier error, partial shipment, or backorder. In any event, the quantity actually received is always entered in this data structure. Since the item number identifies the generic number of the item, it is not necessary to enter this information when the order is received.

The structure presented in Exhibit 5-5 would need to be changed somewhat to work in a traditional multidose system. A new transaction type for credits on returns (if these are to be given) would need to be created. On patientout transaction types, quantity would have to be redefined to allow a higher number. For outpatient pharmacy operations, the patientout transaction would need a field for prescription number.

Supplier Data Structure

As shown in Exhibit 5-6, the supplier data structure is a simple binary tree of records. The binary tree is linked by supplier number. The main function of this structure is to reduce data storage requirements in other data structures related to supply of drugs to the pharmacy. These other structures need store only the supplier number, which is a key to the contents of the supplier data structure. The only other significant function of this structure is to record the time it takes the supplier to deliver items after they have been ordered. The mean delay field is the average number of days between the day the order is mailed and the day the item is delivered to the pharmacy. It is weighted by each item on the order so that it reflects partial shipments. The delaystddev field is the standard deviation of deliveries about the mean, again, in days. Both of these fields are used in the calculation of the EOQ and ERP fields of the inventory file.

This data structure is generally independent of the type of pharmacy system in use. All pharmacies must deal with suppliers of one type or

Exhibit 5-6 Supplier Data Structure

```
Type
  supplierptr              =   ^ supplier;
  Supplier                 =   record
    leftsupplier           :   supplierptr;
    rightsupplier          :   supplierptr;
  . suppliernumber         :   0..9999;
    name                   :   string;
    numberaddr             :   0..4;
    address                :   array [0..numberaddr] of string;
    city                   :   string;
    state                  :   string [0..2];
    zip                    :   0..99999;
    meandelay              :   real;
    delaystddev            :   real
  end; {supplier}
```

Exhibit 5-7 Ordering Data Structure

```
Type
  orderptr                 =   ^ order;
  itemptr                  =   ^ item;
  Order                    :   record
    leftorder              :   orderptr;
    rightorder             :   orderptr;
    ordernumber            :   0..99999999;
    items                  :   itemptr;
    maildate               :   820101..991231
  end; {order}
  Item                     =   record
    nextitem               :   itemptr;
    genericnumber          :   0..99999999;
    suppliernumber         :   0.9999;
    datercvd               :   820101..991231;
    quantity               :   0..999999;
    remainder              :   0..999999
  end; {item}
```

another. It is usually to their advantage to create an orderly structure, such as the one presented, to keep track of them.

Ordering Data Structure

There are two parts to the ordering data structure: order and item (Exhibit 5-7). The order part is a binary tree of records, each of which contains a pointer to the beginning of a list of items. Each item in turn points to the next item on the order. When the last item on a given order is reached, its pointer is nil. The order part contains the order number (by which the binary tree is arranged), the item pointer, and the actual date the order was transmitted to the supplier. The latter makes it possible to calculate turnaround time.

The item part of the structure records data about each item on the order. The item number need not be recorded in the structure, since it is defined by the position of the item in the linked item list. Datercvd is the date on which the entire quantity of the item ordered was received. If partial shipments are received, this field remains empty until the final, completing shipment is received. Quantity is the number of dosage units ordered on the original order. Remainder is the number currently outstanding owing to backorder or partial shipment. When the remainder becomes 0, the current date is put into the datercvd field. When all of the remainders for a given order's items are 0, the order has been completely filled. Procedures should be established to move such orders to storage media for historical (statistical) purposes.

Drug Information Data Structure

In keeping with the increasingly clinical role of the pharmacist, the drug information data structure is rather elaborate (Exhibit 5–8). Maintaining current information in the data base would more than likely consume several full-time equivalent employees (FTEs) of pharmacist time, although it could be argued that maintaining such a data base is the true responsibility of the drug information pharmacist in this day and age. Fortunately, the information in this substructure varies only a little from pharmacy to pharmacy. Thus, a group of pharmacies could arrange to maintain a data base in common. The main items that change from system to system are the generic numbers in the drug formulary structure, the labtest names in the labinteraction structure, and the investigators' names in the investig records.

As shown, the data structure takes advantage of the commonality among drugs in therapeutic categories. The drug locator record identifies for a given generic number the druginfo record that contains information about it. Thus, all the generic numbers for codeine sulfate and codeine phosphate can identify a single file of information. Each druginfo record is a file full of pointers to the specific information related to the therapeutic entity. In most cases, the pointer points to the beginning of a linked list of records. For example, there are usually several chemical names associated with each therapeutic entity. The chemnameptr points to the record called chemname. Each chemname record contains a nextname data item that points to the next chemname on its list. All of the chemnames on the list are

Exhibit 5–8 Drug Information Data Structure

```
Type
    rxptr              = ^druglocator;
    rxinfoptr          = ^druginfo;
    chemnameptr        = ^chemname;
    gennameptr         = ^genname;
    tradenameptr       = ^tradename;
    foreignptr         = ^foreign;
    investigptr        = ^investig;
    misspellingptr     = ^misspelling;
    othernameptr       = ^othername;
    incompatibilityptr = ^incompatibility;
    pkaptr             = ^pka;
    solubilityptr      = ^solubility;
    stabilityptr       = ^stability;
    reconstabilptr     = ^reconstabil;
    indicationptr      = ^indication:
    nonapprovedptr     = ^nonapproved;
    mechanismptr       = ^mechanism;
    cnsactionptr       = ^cnsaction;
    ansactionptr       = ^ansaction;
    hemactionptr       = ^hemaction;
    immunactionptr     = ^immunaction;
    skelactionptr      = ^skelaction;
    endoactionptr      = ^endoaction;
    cardioactionptr    = ^cardioaction;
    gastroactionptr    = ^gastroaction;
    hepactionptr       = ^hepaction;
    muscactionptr      = ^muscaction;
    dermactionptr      = ^dermaction;
    renactionptr       = ^renaction;
    electroactionptr   = ^electroaction;
    neoactionptr       = ^neoaction;
    microactionptr     = ^microaction;
    nutractionptr      = ^nutraction;
    miscactionptr      = ^miscaction;
    allergygrpptr      = ^allergygrp;
    contraindicationptr= ^contraindication;
    teratoptr          = ^terato;
    allergyadrptr      = ^allergyadr;
    uroadrptr          = ^uroadr;
    bloodadrptr        = ^bloodadr;
    senseadrptr        = ^senseadr;
    respadrptr         = ^respadr;
    cnsadrptr          = ^cnsadr;
    addictadrptr       = ^addictadr;
    endoadrptr         = ^endoadr;
    digestadrptr       = ^digestadr;
    hepatadrptr        = ^hepatadr;
```

Exhibit 5–8 continued

```
Type (continued)
    muscadrptr          =   ^muscadr;
    skeladrptr          =   ^skeladr;
    skinadrptr          =   ^skinadr;
    metabadrptr         =   ^metabadr;
    cardioadrptr        =   ^cardioadr;
    miscadrptr          =   ^miscadr;
    adrsummaryptr       =   ^adrsummary;
    oralabsptr          =   ^oralabs;
    distvolptr          =   ^distvol;
    kinmodelptr         =   ^kinmodel;
    peakconIVptr        =   ^peakconIV;
    peakconPOptr        =   ^peakconPO;
    metabsiteptr        =   ^metabsite;
    metabactiveptr      =   ^metabactive;
    halflifenormptr     =   ^halflifenorm;
    halflifeanurptr     =   ^halflifeanur;
    halflifehepptr      =   ^halflifehep;
    TBCnormptr          =   ^TBCnorm;
    TBCanurptr          =   ^TBCanur;
    TBChepptr           =   ^TBChep;
    metabconstptr       =   ^metabconst;
    excrsiteptr         =   ^excrsite;
    excrunchptr         =   ^excrunch;
    excrpHptr           =   ^excrpH;
    excrmiscptr         =   ^excrmisc;
    dialyzptr           =   ^dialyz;
    miscpkinptr         =   ^miscpkin;
    doseadultptr        =   ^doseadult;
    dosepedptr          =   ^doseped;
    therconcptr         =   ^therconc;
    doseparamptr        =   ^doseparam;
    drugintxptr         =   ^drugintx;
    dietintxptr         =   ^dietintx;
    labintxptr          =   ^labintx;
    LD50ptr             =   ^LD50;
    toxdoseptr          =   ^toxdose;
    toxconcptr          =   ^toxconc;
    toxtherptr          =   ^toxther;
    productptr          =   ^product;
    referenceptr        =   ^reference;
    intxgenptr          =   ^intxgen;
    ingredientptr       =   ^ingredient;
Druglocator             =   record
    rightdrug           :   rxptr;
    leftdrug            :   rxptr;
    genericnumber       :   0..99999999;
    location            :   rxinfoptr;
end; {druglocator}
```

Exhibit 5-8 continued

```
Druginfo                        = record
    chemicalnames               : chemnameptr;
    genericnames                : gennameptr;
    BAN                         : string;
    UStradenames                : tradenameptr;
    foreignnames                : foreignptr;
    investigationalnames        : investigptr;
    misspellings                : misspellingptr;
    othernames                  : othernameptr;
    physincompatibilities       : incompatibilityptr;
    solubility                  : solubilityptr;
    dissociationrateconst       : pkaptr;
    stability                   : stabilityptr;
    stabilityreconstituted      : reconstabilptr;
    officialindications         : indicationptr;
    nonapproveduses             : nonapprovedptr;
    mechanismsofaction          : mechanismptr;
    centralnervoussysactions    : cnsactionptr;
    autonomicactions            : ansactionptr;
    hematologicalactions        : hemactionptr;
    immunologicalactions        : immunactionptr;
    skeletalactions             : skelactionptr;
    endocrinologicalactions     : endoactionptr;
    cardiovascularactions       : cardioactionptr;
    gastrointestinalactions     : gastroactionptr;
    hepaticactions              : hepactionptr;
    muscularactions             : muscactionptr;
    dermatologicalactions       : dermactionptr;
    renalactions                : renactionptr;
    electrolyteactions          : electroactionptr;
    actionsonneoplasms          : neoactionptr;
    antimicrobialactions        : microactionptr;
    nutritionaleffects          : nutractionptr;
    miscellaneousactions        : miscactionptr;
    allergygroups               : allergygrpptr;
    contraindications           : contraindicationptr;
    teratogenesis               : teratoptr;
    allergicadr                 : allergyadrptr;
    urogenitaladr               : urogenitaladrptr;
    bloodandlymphadr            : bloodadrptr;
    senseorganadr               : senseadrptr;
    respiratoryadr              : respadrptr;
    psychiatricadr              : psychadrptr;
    centralnervoussystemadr     : cnsadrptr;
    addictivepotential          : addictadrptr;
    endocrineadr                : endoadrptr;
    digestiveadr                : digestadrptr;
    hepaticadr                  : hepatadrptr;
    muscularadr                 : muscadrptr;
```

Exhibit 5-8 continued

```
Druginfo (continued)
    skeletaladr                    :   skeladrptr;
    skinadr                        :   skinadrptr;
    metabolicadr                   :   metabolicadrptr;
    cardiovascularadr              :   cardioadrptr;
    miscellaneousadr               :   miscadrptr;
    adrsummary                     :   adrsummaryptr;
    oralabsorption                 :   oralabsptr;
    distributionvolume             :   distvolptr;
    kineticmodeldescription        :   kinmodelptr;
    IVpeakserumconcentration       :   peakconIVptr;
    POpeakserumconcentration       :   peakconPOptr;
    IMpeakserumconcentration       :   peakconIMptr;
    metabolismsite                 :   metabsiteptr;
    metabolicactivity              :   metabactiveptr;
    halflifenormal                 :   halflifenormptr;
    halflifeanuria                 :   halflifeanurptr;
    halflifehepaticfailure         :   halflifehepptr;
    totalbodyclearancenormal       :   TBCnormptr;
    totalbodyclearanceanuria       :   TBCanurptr;
    totalclearancehepfailure       :   TBChepptr;
    metabolicrateconstant          :   metabconstptr;
    siteofexcretion                :   excrsiteptr;
    urinaryunchexcretionperc       :   excrunchptr;
    urinarypHeffect                :   excrpHptr;
    miscellaneousexcretinfo        :   excrmiscptr;
    dialyzability                  :   dialyzptr;
    miscpharmacokineticinfo        :   miscpkinptr;
    dosageadult                    :   doseadultptr;
    dosagepediatric                :   dosepedptr;
    therapeuticserumconcent        :   therconcptr;
    dosingparameters               :   doseparamptr;
    drugdruginteractions           :   drugintxptr;
    drugdietinteractions           :   dietintxptr;
    druglabtestinteractions        :   labintxptr;
    LD50                           :   LD50ptr;
    toxicdose                      :   toxdoseptr;
    toxicserumconcentration        :   toxconcptr;
    toxicitytherapy                :   toxtherptr;
    productdata                    :   productptr;
end; {druginfo}
Chemname                           =   record
    nextname                       :   chemnameptr;
    chemicalname                   :   string;
end; {chemname}
Genname                            =   record
    nextname                       :   gennameptr;
    genericname                    :   string;
end; {genname}
```

Exhibit 5–8 continued

Tradename	=	record
nextname	:	tradenameptr;
name	:	string;
manufacturer	:	string;
end; {tradename}		
Foreign	=	record
nextname	:	foreignptr;
name	:	string;
country	:	string;
manufacturer	:	string;
end; {foreign}		
Investig	=	record
nextname	:	investigptr;
name	:	string;
manufacturer	:	string;
localchiefinvestigator	:	string;
investigatorphone	:	string;
end; {investig}		
Misspelling	=	record
nextname	:	misspellingptr;
wrongname	:	string;
reference	:	referenceptr;
end; {misspelling}		
Othername	=	record
nextname	:	othernameptr;
name	:	string;
type	:	string;
reference	:	referenceptr;
end; {othername}		
Incompatibility	=	record
nextincompat	:	incompatibilityptr;
genericnumber	:	0..99999999;
description	:	string;
reference	:	referenceptr;
end; {incompatibility}		
Hemaction	=	record
nextaction	:	hemactionptr;
action	:	string;
reference	:	referenceptr;
end; {hemaction}		
Allergygrp	=	record
nextdrug	:	allergygrpptr;
allergygroup	:	integer;
crossreactivity	:	string;
description	:	string;
reference	:	referenceptr;
end; {allergygrp}		

Exhibit 5-8 continued

```
Contraindication                 =  record
   nextcontra                    :     contraindicationptr;
   contradescription             :     string;
   reference                     :     referenceptr;
end; {contraindication}
Terato                           =  record
   nextterat                     :     teratoptr;
   subjectivesymptoms            :     string;
   objectivesymptoms             :     string;
   incidence                     :     string;
   morbidity                     :     string;
   mortality                     :     string;
   reversibility                 :     string;
   mechanism                     :     string;
   predisposingfactors           :     string;
   prevention                    :     string;
   treatment                     :     string;
end; {terato}
Adrsummary                       =  array [1..66] of string;
Oralabs                          =  record
   nextabs                       :     oralabsptr;
   dose                          :     string;
   percentabsorbed               :     string;
   discussion                    :     string;
   reference                     :     referenceptr;
end; {oralabs}
Distvol                          =  record
   nextvol                       :     distvolptr;
   distributionvolume            :     string;
   reference                     :     referenceptr;
end; {distvol}
Drugintx                         =  record
   nextintx                      :     drugintxptr;
   interactiongenericlist        :     intxgenptr;
   description                   :     array [1..5] of string;
   reference                     :     referenceptr;
end; {drugintx}
Intxgen                          =  record
   nextgeneric                   :     intxgenptr;
   genericnumber                 :     0..99999999;
end; {intxgen}
LD50                             =  record
   nextLD                        :     LD50ptr;
   lethaldose                    :     string;
   reference                     :     referenceptr;
end; {LD50}
Reference                        =  record
   author                        :     string;
   title                         :     string;
```

Exhibit 5-8 continued

Reference *(continued)*		
journalname	:	string;
journalvolume	:	integer;
startpage	:	integer;
endpage	:	integer;
datepub	:	0..991231;
end; {reference}		
Ingredient	=	record
nextingred	:	ingredientptr;
ingredient	:	string;
end; {ingredient}		
Product	=	record
nextproduct	:	productptr;
productname	:	string;
manufacturer	:	string;
manufacturerstreet	:	string;
manufacturercitystatezip	:	string;
manufacturerphone	:	1000000000..9999999999;
dateonUSmarket	:	0..991231;
dateoffUSmarket	:	0..991231;
preparationinstructions	:	string;
minIMdilution	:	string;
maxIMdilution	:	string;
minIVdilution	:	string;
maxIVdilution	:	string;
administrationrate	:	string;
dosageform	:	string;
administrationroute	:	string;
administrationinstruct	:	string;
ingredients	:	ingredientptr;
end; {product}		

associated with the same therapeutic entity. When a nextname with a value of nil is found, the end of the list has been reached. The tradename and foreign records are the same, except that they include a string for the manufacturer's name and, in the case of foreign, country of manufacture. The investig record is similar but includes the name and telephone number of the local investigator. Institutions that handle many investigational drugs would probably want a much more elaborate investig record, listing the telephone numbers and names of all approved investigators; however, most of the information usually collected by a pharmacy to monitor investigational drugs (e.g., symptoms of toxicity, special instructions for administration) is already part of the data structure demonstrated.

The misspelling record is the first record to make use of the reference pointer. In many cases, it is not sufficient to know, for example, that the half-life of a drug is a given numeric value. In this case, it is desirable to be able to locate the original research that led to this conclusion. The reference pointer points to the journal citation from which the data were derived. The way the reference record is shown in this structure (near the end of the structure) only one reference may be linked to a given record. The fact that several separate information records can point to the same reference record conserves memory, but it would be useful to be able to cite a list of references for each information record by having the pointer point to a linked list. This would make it impossible to reuse the reference records, however, since each would be a part of a unique linked list.

The misspelling record contains a common misspelling of the drug's name, for example, "propanolol" for propranolol. This would emphasize misspellings commonly found in the literature by citing the reference. The othername record contains a name that does not fit under any of the categories that have been described. This is primarily for common names, such as ASA for aspirin or nitroglycerin for glyceryl trinitrate.

The incompatibility record is the first of a series of records that contain information about the physical properties of drugs. Since the structure of these records is very similar, only one is shown in Exhibit 5-8. The genericnumber is a reference to the drug with which the drug in question is incompatible. The description should include temperature, concentration, and other conditions up to 255 characters. In solubility, the genericnumber is replaced with the diluent name.

The hemaction record is the first of a series of records to store information about the activity of drugs. These records are configured as linked lists. All of the hematological actions of a drug, for example, are found in a linked list beginning at the record pointed to by the record in druginfo. The list continues as pointed to by nextaction until nextaction has a value of nil. Since all of the action records have essentially the same structure, only the first example is shown in Exhibit 5-8.

The allergygrp record is also a linked list. This record serves as a link between allergically cross-reacting drugs. For the purpose of checking patients' potential allergies, all drugs in the drug information file are assigned to a series of allergy groups. Each allergy group is assigned an integer number. Since many drugs exhibit allergic cross-reaction with several drugs, the linked list contains all the allergy groups of which the drug in question is a part. Whenever a patient shows an allergy to a drug, the patient record structure is annotated with all of the allergy group numbers appropriate to that drug. The crossreactivity field describes the relative certainty of an allergic reaction in a person allergic to this drug when given another drug in this group. Description is a summary of research on this drug's allergic nature. A reference is also in the record.

After the contraindication record, the terato record appears. This is the first of a series of records that document any adverse drug reaction (adr) seen with the entity in question. These records have an extended internal structure to assist the health care practitioner in diagnosis, assessment, and treatment of adverse drug reactions. The structure is a linked list containing descriptions of reported reactions in the given area (e.g., teratogenetic dermatological) for the entity in question. Only the first example is shown in Exhibit 5–8, since all the adverse reaction records are essentially the same. The adr summary record is a one-page (66-line) summary of adverse reactions observed with the entity.

Oralabs is the first of another series of records. This series documents published pharmacokinetics of drugs. A linked list, its structure and that of distvol are straightforwardly shown in Exhibit 5–8. Only two examples are shown for the sake of brevity.

Drugintx is a record used to check for therapeutic interactions between drugs that a patient is taking concurrently. Since most interactions can be expected to occur with more than one other drug, interactiongenericlist is a pointer to a linked list of generic numbers for drugs implicated in the interaction. The description field allows five strings of summary regarding the interaction. A reference pointer is also included. Dietintx and labintx, which are not shown in Exhibit 5–8, are the same as drugintx, except that they point to a list of standard diet/food names or labtest names instead of a generic number.

LD50, which stands for the lethal dose per kilogram (in 50 percent of test animals) for the drug in question, is the first of a series of records that document the toxicology of drugs. Like others that have been described, these are linked lists with a string description and a reference pointer.

The final record of this example data structure contains product-specific information. It is organized as a linked list of all the products manufactured in the United States that contain the drug referenced in the druginfo record that points to it. There are usually several such products. Productname is the complete trade name, especially including any description of the dosage form. Dosage form is also captured as a separate string. Manufacturer's name, address, and telephone number are included because the manufacturer may not necessarily be in the supplier file, and it is occasionally necessary to contact the manufacturer for emergency information about a product. Memory can be conserved by using a supplier pointer here and creating dummy supplier entries—entries in the supplier file for manufacturers who are not actually the pharmacy's supplier for the item. The dates on and off the U.S. market are recorded to answer the frequently asked questions, "Is X still on the market?" and "Is Y on the market yet?" Historical files of such information are also useful in determining in utero or neonatal exposure to potential teratogens or carcinogens, since one of the most difficult problems in such investigations is usually just to determine the composition of a discontinued product.

Instructions for preparing the product for patient administration are most commonly used to describe parenteral product dilution or reconstitution. The minimum and maximum intravenous (IV) and intramuscular (IM) dilution recommendations are included. Administration rate, route, and instructions are captured as strings. Ingredients is a pointer to a linked list of all the ingredients in the product. Whenever released by the manufacturer, this information includes all constituents of the product, including excipients, binders, and colorants. The structure of this linked list is straightforward. If there are to be druginfo records for each ingredient of any product in the file, the drug name should exactly match the string used in the ingredient record.

ALGORITHMS

If the data structure was inserted as described earlier and the procedures referenced were written, the program shown in Exhibit 5-9 would run. Treeread, the first procedure referenced, is a hypothetical procedure that gathers information from mass storage and sets up the dynamic binary trees and linked lists in the data structure. These structures would have been converted into files of arrays and records when the system was last powered down, and this reconversion is necessary because pointers cannot be written to mass storage or printed. Before the first use of the system, dummy files must be created to prevent the program from terminating when it tries to read from nonexistent files. Treeread is a very complex procedure. With certain types of computer systems, it might be worthwhile to save the entire contents of memory in mass storage, thereby keeping the pointer structure intact. This procedure, called treeread here, is most likely to be useful on a small, single user system. Treeread and treesave would take hours in a typical system. Treeread has no parameters and, by its very nature, must create all the data structures as global (affecting the entire program).

The next construct is a REPEAT-UNTIL EOF statement. Between the REPEAT and UNTIL are a series of WRITELN commands that present a menu to the user via the CRT screen. Since these choices represent everything the system can do, this is called the main menu. The user selects which action is to be performed by pressing a single key on the keyboard. This key is the same as the letter that was capitalized in the menu choice. The CASE statement selects the appropriate procedure to perform. When the user is finished performing that procedure, control returns to this RE-

Exhibit 5-9 Pseudocode for Main Pharmacy Program

```
Program Pharmacy (input, output);
Type
  {as previously defined}
Var
  {as previously defined plus}
  mainselection                    :  (N,n,C,c,F,f,R,r,
                                        P,p,M,m,D,d,G,g,B,b);
Begin
  treeread;
  repeat
    writeln ('select one:');
    writeln ('New patient order');
    writeln ('Cancel patient order');
    writeln ('Fill patient order');
    writeln ('Returned carts');
    writeln ('Purchasing functions');
    writeln ('Move stock');
    writeln ('Database changes');
    writeln ('Generate report');
    writeln ('Bid system');
    read (mainselection);
    case mainselection of
      n,N                          :  neworder;
      c,C                          :  cancelorder;
      f,F                          :  fillorder;
      r,R                          :  cartreturn;
      p,P                          :  purchasing;
      m,M                          :  movestock;
      d,D                          :  changedatabase;
      g,G                          :  report;
      b,B                          :  bids;
      otherwise                    :  writeln ('Please make another choice')
    end; {case}
  UNTIL EOF;
  treesave;
end. {pharmacy}
```

PEAT loop, causing the menu to appear again. Thus the program continues running until the EOF becomes true, usually when user presses the return key in response to the main menu. Depending on the operating system, an empty input line (return only) may be the definition given to EOF for interactive jobs. It might be desirable in some systems to assign the UNTIL condition to a value that can be affected only by the system operator from the console. This would prevent inadvertent temporary shutdown of the system.

When EOF occurs, the program calls procedure treesave. When the data structures have been recorded on mass storage (disk and backup tape), the program ends, and control returns to the operating system of the computer. A regular schedule by which the system is backed up is implemented by the administrator in charge of the computer.

Service Procedures

Some procedures that perform common routines needed over and over throughout a program are service procedures. For example, binsearch takes two parameters and returns one. The two input parameters are the name of the data structure to search and the key value to find. The returned parameter is a pointer to the record containing the key value. The biggest problem in writing such a procedure is writing it to work with any of several different data structures. A case construct may be used to specify which data structure is to be searched. Structure-specific information indicates the search routine to be used. Searching is done by traversing the tree, looking at left and right key values based on whether the search key is greater than or less than the record value being examined. When the first key that matches in the first n characters, where n is the length of the key being sought, is found, the pointer is returned.

Bindelete is a procedure to delete a record from a binary tree data structure. The parameters are the key value identifying the record to be deleted and the name of the data structure from which to delete it. As mentioned earlier, this is a complex procedure. Suffice it to say that, after using a case construct to identify the appropriate data structure, this procedure uses binsearch to find the key for deletion and deletes it. It then writes the record's contents onto a transaction type file on tape to allow historical reconstruction of the data structure at a future date. This can be very important for retrospective chronic drug toxicity studies.

Binadd is the opposite of bindelete; it adds a record to a binary tree data structure. The parameter entered is the name of the data structure. Binadd first uses a case construct to determine the specific processing required for the data structure chosen. For each structure, a writeln and readln series solicits the information needed for the record. This information is inserted into a new record by means of the Pascal "new" intrinsic function. After each readln, range and error checking are performed. If an error is found, the information is resolicited. Conditional branching code is incorporated to accommodate variants of dynamic data structures. When the new record is complete, the record is inserted into the chosen structure by comparison of its key value with that of the keys already in the tree. The pointer is then stored in the appropriate right or left pointer of the record in the structure. The record thus becomes a de facto part of the data structure, and binadd is finished, except for creating a transaction type record on tape, just as in bindelete.

Bindump is a procedure to list out a number of records from a binary tree in alphabetic order, beginning at a given key value. The parameters are the data structure name, the key value to begin with, and the number of records to print. Bindump uses a case construct to find the data structure specified, uses binsearch to locate the first occurrence of the beginning key in the data structure, prints this record, and then enters a DO loop that repeats one less time than the number of records requested via the parameter. This loop traverses the tree printing leftmost records as they are found until the correct number have been printed.

Four other procedures perform the same processes on linked list data structures: linksearch, linkdelete, linkadd, and linkdump. Although these procedures are much simpler to write, they make less efficient use of the computer's resources. Linked lists are used in the data structure only when binary trees would not work or would unnecessarily increase the memory requirements.

Working Procedures

The pseudocode for neworder, a procedure to process new orders, is shown in Exhibit 5–10. It in turn calls several procedures. The first procedure, authorize, solicits the user's authority level, which may be technician, intern, pharmacist (rph), or system. It checks a password to be certain that the person really has the authority claimed. If the correct password is not given, the user is returned to the main pharmacy program. The parameter returned is status the authority level allowed. Only pharmacists, for instance, may check orders and only system authority may modify inventory records. The rest of the procedure repeats until the user terminates it by striking two carriage returns in a row or enters a control c, depending on how the operating system defines the EOF condition.

Getname solicits the patient's name, which may be done in many different ways. One of the most popular, owing to its efficiency, is to ask the question and then read a string. The string may be any part of a name. A search is then performed for the name by means of a subroutine, such as bindump. This displays a screenful of records with the first occurrence of the string requested. The user then chooses one of these records by number or asks the system for the next "page" of records. Since the system knows the pointer to the first record, it can trace the tree n more records forward, where n is the choice number input by the user. Getdrug is a very similar procedure that produces a generic number.

A Hypothetical Pharmacy System 139

Exhibit 5-10 Procedure Neworder

```
Procedure neworder (Var nameptr : patient;
                        genericnumber : 0..99999999;
                        warning : boolean;
                        status : statustype;
                        warnptr : ptrwarn;
Type
Var
Begin
  authorize (status);
  While not EOF DO
    begin
      getname (nameptr);
      getdrug (genericnumber);
      intxsearch (nameptr, genericnumber, warning, warnptr);
      if warning
        then warn(warnptr);
      if status = rph or status = system
        then binadd (Rx)
    end; {while}
end; {neworder}
```

Intxsearch is a procedure to check automatically whether the newly ordered drug would interact with any of the other drugs the patient is taking or any labtests that have been performed at the time the order is entered. It also scans the diet interaction file for the drug and inserts a note in the patient record if the drug is known to interact with any food or diet. It is then up to the medical staff to make certain that the patient's diet is controlled. The parameters sent to intxsearch are the pointer to the patient's record and the generic number obtained earlier. The parameters returned are warning, which is boolean (true or false) and warnptr, which points to a linked list of warning messages.

In performing the drug interaction portion of the search, intxsearch performs a binsearch on the drug locator record for every drug in the patient's current drug order list. After each one it uses rxinfoptr to find the drugintxptr that points to the first record of the linked list of generic numbers for drugs that interact with the currently ordered drug. If the generic number of the newly ordered drug appears on this list, then warning is set to true, and warnptr points to the drug interaction record. The search then continues with the next drug on the patient's current order list. When all orders have been thus checked, the procedure ends. A very similar procedure is followed for labtest and diet interactions. With diet interactions, there is no list of foods or diets in the patient record. The search is performed on the new drug being ordered; warning is set true if that drug interacts with any food or diet.

If the warning flag has been set to true, then procedure neworder calls procedure warn. Warn looks at the drug interaction pointers and prints out the text of the drug interaction files for the drugs involved. If the user wants the references after each record, they can be read and displayed by means of the referenceptr in the interaction record. A copy of the messages can be printed, if desired. When all of the intx records have been displayed, warn is finished.

When the program returns to neworder, a new order is solicited by the binadd procedure. When binadd is finished, neworder goes back to the WHILE statement and repeats everything other than authorize.

For other hospital pharmacy systems, the major alteration necessary in neworder would be in the specific binadd routine that updates the data structure. This would have to be customized to the data structure of the individual hospital.

Exhibit 5–11 presents the pseudocode for cancelorder, the second procedure called from the main pharmacy program. Instead of actually deleting a canceled order from the structure, this procedure changes the lastdose field of the order to a nonzero value. This cancels the order but allows the information to remain in the data structure for historical use in patient management.

Authorize and getname are the same procedures used in neworder; getorder is a very similar procedure. Getorder returns drugptr, a pointer to the specific record that contains the order to be canceled. It takes nameptr from getname. Many different means can be used to accomplish the getorder procedure. One popular and efficient way is to solicit a drugname string and search it for the patient's Rxbase pointer and Rx records.

Exhibit 5–11 Cancelorder Procedure

```
Procedure Cancelorder; {field list, variable declarations, etc.}
Begin
  authorize (status);
  while not EOF do
    begin
      getname (nameptr);
      getorder (nameptr, drugptr);
      writeln ('Time of last dose?');
      readln (time);
      drugptr^.lastdose = time;
    end; {while}
end; {cancelorder}
```

When the order to be canceled is located, the user indicates its number on the screen, and the procedure returns with its pointer. This type of cancelorder procedure works for most hospital pharmacy systems, because orders are generally considered continuous unless otherwise specified.

The third procedure called from the main pharmacy program is procedure fillorder (Exhibit 5–12). Unless it is notified otherwise, the system assumes that every dose ordered gets to the patient. Thus, a cart fill list can be printed or displayed for any arbitrary period of time a user specifies to it. This can lead to occasional problems, however, if a user carelessly enters the wrong dates for the fill list. Range checking on dates and times can be easily installed if desired, but it would, of course, disallow printing of a fill list for any date not starting with the current date or later. Furthermore, it would be impossible to monitor clinical therapy by asking the system for last week's therapy on a patient (by specifying startroom and lastroom as their room number) on a fill list system employing range checking.

Fillorder initially solicits the first and last room numbers, dates, and times, using standard readln and writeln statements. It then calls sort, which

Exhibit 5–12 Order-Filling Procedure

```
Procedure Fillorder; {field list, variables, etc.}
Begin
   authorize (status);
   writeln ('Starting room number?');
   readln (startroom);
   writeln ('Last room number?');
   readln (lastroom);
   writeln ('Time starting?');
   readln (starttime);
   writeln ('Date starting?');
   readln (startdate);
   writeln ('Time ending?');
   readln (lasttime);
   writeln ('Date ending?');
   readln (lastdate);
   sort (roomptr);
   search (startroom, roomptr);
   cartprint (roomptr, lastroom, startdate, starttime, lastdate, lasttime);
   IVprint (roomptr, lastroom, startdate, starttime, lastdate, lasttime);
end; {fillorder}
```

creates a sort key in the form of a linked list of pointers to the patient record structure:

```
Type
    roomptr = ^ room;
    nameptr = ^ patient;
    room    = record;
        nextroom : roomptr;
        patient  : nameptr;
    end; {room}
```

This sort key gives the sorted order of the patient's hospital room number by the position of its pointer on the linked list. This list must be recreated each time a cartfill list is to be produced in order to accommodate admission, discharge, and transfer changes. Fillorder then calls search and passes it the startroom as a parameter. Search finds the location of the first room in the range selected and returns its pointer as roomptr. Fillorder then calls cartlist and IVlist. Cartlist takes roomptr, lastroom, starttime, lasttime, startdate, and lastdate as parameters and produces a list in numeric order by room number of the name, number, and strength of each dosage form necessary to fill the cart for the period specified by the parameters. This is usually done on paper so that an initialed copy can be maintained for record-keeping purposes. The person in charge of filling the cart refers to this list while filling the cart. The checker does likewise.

In some operations, a preliminary report is generated to allow the filler first to customize the pick area by listing all of the drugs that will be needed. These are then placed in order in the pick area, reducing fill time. Fillorder also checks serial lot numbers of all drugs being dispensed to see if any have expired. IVlist performs a very similar action, except that it prints only compound drugs, listing the ingredients needed for each. A similar preliminary report might be used by IV additive personnel to prepare solutions in advance.

When IVlist is finished, fillorder terminates and control returns to the main program. As described, fillorder works only with a unit dose, cartfill system with pharmacy only additive manufacture. A traditional multidose hospital pharmacy needs a completely different scheme for filling and refilling orders. Each transaction must be explicitly entered into the system. A file of refills is necessary, implying a different data structure.

The cartreturn procedure (Exhibit 5–13) is run whenever a cart exchange or refill operation is performed. In this system, accounting and billing are performed at this point. The first procedure called by cartreturn is authorize, important for security purposes. As it does in the order-filling

Exhibit 5-13 Cartreturn Procedure

```
Procedure Cartreturn; {field list, variable declarations, etc.}
Begin
    authorize (status);
    sort (roomptr);
    getcart (startroom, lastroom, startdate, lastdate, starttime, lasttime);
    search (startroom, roomptr);
    getreturns (startroom, lastroom, startdate, lastdate, starttime, lasttime, returnptr,
            roomptr);
    recordchange (returnptr);
    transaction (startroom, lastroom, startdate, lastdate, starttime, lasttime, returnptr,
            roomptr);
    inventory (startroom, lastroom, startdate, lastdate, starttime, lasttime, returnptr,
            roomptr)
end; {cartreturn}
```

procedure, sort creates a list of the patients by room number. Roomptr points to the beginning of this list. Because sort uses the current admission, discharge, and transfer file in doing this, the drug bin must move with patients who change rooms so that their drug therapy information will follow them. Obviously, admission, discharge, and transfer information must be absolutely current before procedure cartreturn is called.

Getcart solicits the data regarding the cart being returned. This procedure can be designed to fit real carts within the hospital and the actual schedule of cart exchanging in use. The cart data are passed to a search procedure, which returns a pointer to the first room that belongs to the cart. Getreturns then works through the cart, presenting each patient's name, the drug item, and the number that should have been sent. It solicits the number returned with the cart. If the number is not 0, getreturns creates a record of the patient, drug, quantity, date, and time returned; this is on a temporary linked list pointed to by returnptr. When all the patients who had medication on the cart have been worked through, recordchange takes the pointer to the list of returned items and updates the patient records involved.

The transaction procedure then creates a file entry for each group of doses used by a patient. This entry is made on tape—or directly on another mass storage device. Periodically, the tape is copied, and the copy serves as a charging document for the accounting system. Any preprocessing necessary for this file depends on the specific hospital billing system in use. The inventory procedure updates the system's inventory files based on the numbers and types of items not returned (and therefore used by the patient). This procedure involves an internal routine that uses the transaction file to update the mean use rate, ERP, and EOQ of the inventory data structure. The portion of the transaction file to be used in these calculations is defined by the system administrator and should be several days to a week. Another internal routine in the inventory procedure checks for potentially expired drugs in the cost center responsible for the cart. A list of serial groups to be checked is printed. When everything has been posted to inventory, control returns to the main program.

Cartreturn works only in a unit dose system. Completely different concepts must be used to account for drugs dispensed in other types of pharmacy systems. A nonsatellite unit dose system, which has only one cost center, requires a simple modification in a system designed for satellite pharmacies.

Exhibit 5–14 presents the procedure for handling purchasing. After status has been checked by authorize, one of three primary functions can be used. Based on this selection, purchasing either uses binadd to create a new order or calls a procedure, such as the receivestock procedure. This procedure first calls getorderno, which solicits information about the order that has arrived in the pharmacy and locates the order in the order data structure. It returns orderpoint, a pointer to the order in that structure. It then calls getdate, producing an integer variable called date. Receivestock then calls listorder to produce a printed copy of the order. Listorder uses binsearch to find the order and linkdump to print or display it. The person receiving stock uses this as an aid in inventorying the items received.

The next structure solicits and processes each item on the order in sequence by item number (really, its position on the linked list). Getitem advances the itemnopointer to the next item of the order. Orderpoint tells it which order has the item. The procedure then solicits the number of dosage forms received as quantity, an integer. Inventory then updates the inventory data structure after it gets the generic number of the item received from the item field of the order data structure. Serialize creates new serial groups, using, in part, the binadd procedure. Suppliers then updates the mean time to deliver for this item, using the date given by getdate. Transact then records this as a stocking type of transaction on the transaction file tape. When the end of the item list is reached, control returns to the purchasing program and then the main program.

If the mailorder procedure is selected from purchasing, getdate is called first for the current date. Getorderno then solicits information about the order to be mailed out and, after searching the order file, returns its pointer as orderpoint. Bindump is then called to print the order onto a standard order form that is positioned in the printer. After this, or perhaps while printing is in progress, supplierupdate is called to update the supplier data structure with the date mailed. This allows mean time to delivery to be

Exhibit 5-14 Purchasing Procedure

```
Procedure Purchasing; {field list, variable declarations, etc.}
Begin:
    authorize (status);
    writeln ('Select one:');
    writeln ('Receive stock');
    writeln ('Create orders');
    writeln ('Mail orders');
    read (selection);
    case selection of
        R,r                      :   receivestock (status);
        C,c                      :   binadd (order);
        M,m                      :   mailorder;
    end; {case}
end; {purchasing}

Procedure Receivestock; {field list, variable declarations, etc.}
Begin
    getorderno (orderpoint);
    getdate (date);
    listorder (orderpoint);
    repeat
        getitem (quantity, orderpoint, itemno);
        inventory (quantity, orderpoint, itemno);
        serialize (quantity, orderpoint, itemno);
        suppliers (quantity, orderpoint, itemno);
        transact (quantity, orderpoint, itemno);
    until itemno^.nextitem = nil;
end; {receivestock}

Procedure Mailorder; {field list, variable declarations, etc.}
Begin
    getdate (date);
    getorderno (orderpoint);
    bindump (order, order.orderno^orderpoint, 1);
    supplierupdate (orderpoint, date);
end; {mailorder}
```

determined. When this is completed, control returns to the purchasing procedure.

Exhibit 5-15 presents the procedure to move stock from one cost center to another. After invoking authorize, movestock uses getdate. It then calls getserial, which solicits the serial group number and generic number of the item to be transferred. Getcenter solicits the center that is to receive the serial group. The system already knows which cost center has the item. Transactmove then creates a transaction file record. Changecenter changes

Exhibit 5–15 Cost Center Stock Moving Procedure

```
Procedure Movestock; {field list, variable declarations, etc.}
Begin
    getdate (date);
    authorize (status);
    getserial (serialgroupptr);
    getcenter (centerout);
    transactmove (serialgroupptr, centerout, date, serialgroupptr^.costcenter;
    changecenter (date, serialgroupptr);
end; {movestock}
```

the cost center field and calls the routines to calculate mean use rate, ERP, and EOQ. Control is then returned to the main program.

Data base management procedures are presented in Exhibit 5–16. Changedatabase is a general purpose procedure to allow modification of the data structure in the pharmacy. Authorize allows only professional staff to access this feature. Entry of data such as patient medical records, drug information records, and formulary entries is achieved through this procedure. Since the binadd and bindelete procedures create transaction files on tape, all changes to the file are recorded permanently. Changedatabase first solicits the type of operation to be performed and then solicits the filename on which the operation is to be performed. Filename is passed to each of the procedures in the case construct.

The root level of all the data structures is a binary tree, except for the transaction file. This allows the construct to use the "bin" procedures unless the filename is transactions. For the transaction file there are some analogous "trans" files: transadd, transsearch, and transdump. There is no transdelete procedure, however, since this would be analogous to erasing from the patient's medical record and would defeat the purpose of a transaction file. Because negatives are allowed, the effect of deleting can be achieved by adding an opposing transaction.

Transdump produces a loosely formatted copy of the entire file that has no headings and is mainly intended for use as a data base maintenance document. When the selected procedure is done, control returns to the main program. At this level, no modification of changedatabase would be necessary for it to run in any pharmacy systems; however, the lower level procedures would need to be customized to accommodate variations in the data base owing to the system type.

After calling authorize, the report generator procedure presents a two-item selection and uses a case construct to select which action to take (Exhibit 5–17). If the choice is to create a new report definition, then report calls getstructure, which solicits the name of the structure(s) from

A Hypothetical Pharmacy System 147

Exhibit 5-16 Data Base Management Procedures

```
Procedure Changedatabase; {field list, variable declaration, etc.}
Begin
    authorize (status);
    writeln ('Select one:');
    writeln ('Add to a data structure');
    writeln ('Delete from a data structure');
    writeln ('Search a data structure');
    writeln ('Entire structure dump');
    read (selection);
    getfilename (filename);
    case selection of
        A,a : if filename = transactions
                    then transadd;
                    else binadd (filename);
        D,d : if filename = transactions
                    then writeln ('transactions are never deleted. Add an opposing transaction');
                    else
                        begin
                            getkey (filename, key);
                            bindelete (filename, key)
                        end; {else}
        S,s : if filename = transactions
                    then transsearch;
                    else
                        begin
                            getkey (filename, key);
                            binsearch (filename, key, 1);
                            printkey (filename, key, 1)
                        end; {else}
        E,e : if filename = transactions
                    then transdump;
                    else bindump (filename, all);
    end; {case}
end; {changedatabase}
```

which data for the report will be obtained. This is passed as the variable structurename. The procedure then repeatedly solicits the names of fields (and data structures, if more than one) to be included in the report until the user terminates the list with an EOF. These are placed in order on a linked list pointed to by fieldnamepoint. Report then solicits a name for the report, using getreportname, and adds the report to reportfile, a binary tree structure using binadd. The report writing procedure can print a report based on data thus collected.

The second choice of the case is to print a report. If this is chosen, getreportname solicits the name of the report to be printed and then calls

Exhibit 5–17 Report Generator Procedure

```
Procedure Report; {field list, variable declarations, etc.}
Begin
    writeln ('Select one:');
    writeln ('Create report definition');
    writeln ('Print existing report');
    read (selection);
    case selection of
       C,c : begin
                getstructure (structurename);
                while not eof do
                    getfieldname (structurename, fieldnamepoint);
                getreportname (reportname);
                binadd (reportfile)
              end; {create definition}
       P,p : begin
                getreportname (reportname);
                binsearch (reportfile, reportname, pointer);
                reportwrite (pointer)
             end; {existing report}
        end; {case}
end; {report}
```

binsearch to locate the pointer to the report description. Reportwrite then takes this pointer and repetitively prints the data structure value in its corresponding column until the end of the data structure is reached. A sampling of the typical reports a pharmacy would need includes

- drug utilization review
- nonformulary drug use
- current budgetary commitment
- value of inventory
- turnover of inventory
- bid invitation data
- pick area setup list
- expired drugs
- inventory indicating drugs near ERP

Again, at this level, there would be no modification necessary in the system for it to work in any pharmacy setting, although it may be necessary to adapt the lower level procedures for the specific data structure installed.

Appendix A
Glossary

appendix A

Accumulator—The part of a computer that holds data while they are manipulated by the CPU.

Acoustic coupler—A communication device that converts audible sounds into an electrical communication signal.

Addend—A number being added to another number.

Address—The identifier of the location of a byte of memory, usually a binary number.

Address space—The numeric size of memory that can be addressed at the same time by a CPU.

A/D interface—*See* analog to digital interface.

Algorithm—A step-by-step procedure for finding the solution to a problem.

ALU—*See* arithmetic and logic unit.

American Standard Code for Information Interchange—A coding scheme that provides binary equivalents for alphabetic, numeric, control, and punctuational characters. It is the officially recognized standard used by the majority of computer manufacturers.

Analog—Information that can be divided into an infinite number of steps. Opposite of digital.

Analog to digital interface—An electronic circuit that converts analog electrical currents into digital information that a computer can process.

Arithmetic and logic unit—The section of a CPU that contains the electronic circuits for Boolean, arithmetic, and shifting operations.

Array—A data structure in which similar data elements are given the same mnemonic. Each specific datum is identified by its numeric order in the array.

ASCII—*See* American Standard Code for Information Interchange.

Assembler—A computer program that converts a file of mnemonic instruction codes, operands, and sometimes comments into an object code program that a computer can perform.

Asynchronous serial communication—A mode of serial communication in which a computer transmits material only when data are available.

Banked memory—Memory that is divided into banks, only one of which can be connected at a time.

Base—The control input of a transistor.

Batch mode—A mode of computer operation in which programs are stored in a queue and performed as convenient for the computer system.

Baud rate—The number of bits per second in a communication channel.

BCD—*See* binary coded decimal.

Benchmark—A short repetitive program written to determine the capability of a system to perform work intended for it. The time taken by the system to perform the benchmark program is considered indicative of the speed with which it will perform the desired tasks.

Binary coded decimal—A system of numbers in which four-bit codes are associated with each decimal number.

Binary mathematics—The branch of mathematics that performs all operations using only 1s and 0s.

Bit—A contraction of binary digit; either 0 or 1.

Boolean logic—A system of logic based upon the operators AND, OR, EOR, and NOT.

Bootstrapping—The process the computer goes through when it is first turned on to load a program (monitor) that instructs it to read a device, usually a keyboard, and follow instructions received from the device.

Branching instructions—Instructions that modify the contents of the PC register, causing the program to change the sequence of instructions.

Byte—An arbitrarily defined size of a set of bits that is given a systematic interpretation through a code conversion table. In most microcomputers, a byte is the same as the word size, which is eight bits. Unless the context indicates that there is an exception, a byte is eight bits.

Calculator—A computing machine that operates in an immediate mode and deals exclusively with numeric characters.

Central processing unit—The central part of a computer that performs the actual manipulation of data. It is composed of the arithmetic and logic unit (ALU), the microprogramming section, the internal bus, and the special processing registers.

Clock—The portion of a computer that sets the pace for the rest of the system by sending out a signal at a regular time interval.

Collector—The part of a transistor that forms the input path.

COM—*See* computer output microfiche.

Compiler—A computer program that converts (compiles) a file of valid commands from a specific computer language into an object code file that a computer can run from beginning to end.

Complement—The number that, when added to a given number, gives the base of the number system.

Computer—An electronic machine capable of performing arithmetic and Boolean operations, as well as memory moves and shifts, in a delayed (stored program) mode and that handles alphabetic, numeric, control, and punctuational information.

Computer literacy—An emerging educational concept related to training or retraining the population to cope with the computer revolution.

Computer output microfiche—Microfiche produced by a computer device without manual intervention.

Constant—A data structure in which a permanent numeric value is assigned to a mnemonic.

Controller—An electronic circuit that attaches to the bus of a central processing unit (CPU) through specially designed interfacing slots and controls the operation of peripheral device, such as a disk drive.

Core—Ferrite core memory.

CPS—Characters per second.

CPU—*See* central processing unit.

CRT—Cathode ray terminal or cathode ray tube.

Current—Flow of electricity (electrons) in electrical circuits that, when present, usually signifies the 1 digit in computer circuits.

D/A converters—*See* digital to analog converters.

Data structure—A programming device for keeping track of data or information in a computer program.

DB25—The standard connector for RS232-compatible devices.

Decimal mathematics—The common base 10 system of mathematics used in everyday scientific and business calculations.

Decrement—Decrease by 1.

Digital—The opposite of analog. Digital systems divide information into discrete steps and cannot deal with values between the steps. Digital values are typified by 1, 2, 3, 4, 5, etc.; analog values have an infinite number of steps between 1 and 2, between 2 and 3, etc.

Digital to analog converters—An electronic circuit that converts digital computer information into an analog electrical current.

Digitization—*See* video digitizers.

Direct addressing—A memory-addressing mode in which the two bytes of the address being referenced are placed immediately after the memory move instruction.

Direct memory access—A technique used by many systems in which the contents of memory are moved directly from one location to another, without going through the central processing unit (CPU).

Disk—A flat, circular magnetized device used to store information.

Dividend—In division, the number being divided.

Divisor—In division, the dividing number.

DMA—*See* direct memory access.

Documentation—Information about a computer program that assists in its maintenance or repair. Sometimes documentation is included in the program.

Duplex—The status of a communication channel with regard to two-way communication. Full duplex signifies full simultaneous two-way communication. Half duplex signifies one-way communication, i.e., the devices alternate.

Dynamic random access memory (RAM)—RAM that slowly loses its contents and must be periodically refreshed.

EBCDIC—*See* extended binary coded decimal information code.

Emitter—The path of a transistor that forms the output path.

Encoder—An electronic circuit that converts a single key stroke into the appropriate binary code pattern.

EPROM—*See* erasable programmable read only memory.

Erasable programmable read only memory—Memory that may be programmed by simple circuits available in many computers and that may be totally, repeatedly erased by exposure of the circuit to ultraviolet light.

Appendix A 155

Extended binary coded decimal information code—A coding scheme that provides binary equivalents for alphabetic, numeric, control, and punctuational characters. It is not an accepted standard code and is used mainly by IBM equipment.

Fiche—*See* microfiche.

Field—The smallest elemental part of a record that contains a single datum. Fields usually have a fixed size in number of bytes.

File—A sequential data structure composed of records.

Firmware—Computer programs on read only memory (ROM).

Flag register—A part of the CPU containing bits that may be tested by certain instructions to control program flow and that are modified by certain instructions.

Flexible diskette—A disk made of plastic and coated with a magnetic material. These are removable.

Floppy disk—*See* flexible diskette.

F register—*See* flag register.

Function—A mathematically defined set of procedures to be performed on the operand(s) whenever the function name is invoked. Some computer languages allow users to define their own functions.

Hand-shaking signals—Communication signals that determine which device will send, which will receive, and whether or not each device is ready. Sometimes a signal to acknowledge receipt of data is included.

Hardware—Electronic components that comprise a computer.

Hexadecimal numbers—Numbers written in base 16, which correspond to all of the possible permutations of four bits.

Immediate addressing—Direct addressing.

Increment—Increase by 1.

Indexed addressing—A memory-addressing mode in which the address is determined by adding the next byte to the contents of one or more register(s).

Input/output interface—Any interface between devices outside the central processing unit (CPU) and the CPU, other than the system bus.

Internal bus—A set of electronic paths in the central processing unit (CPU) that facilitate movement of data in the CPU.

Interpreter—A computer program that converts (interprets) a file of valid commands from a specific computer language into object code on a line-by-line basis. It performs each line immediately after interpreting it.

Interrupt—An electronic signal that causes the central processing unit (CPU) to stop working and perform a specific routine.

Invert—To perform the NOT operation on a set of binary bits.

I/O interface—*See* input/output interface.

LCD—*See* liquid crystal display.

Least significant bit—*See* significance.

LED—*See* light emitting diode.

Light emitting diode—An electronic device that gives off light and is used to display information stored in computers.

Liquid crystal display—A low-energy electronic device that is used to display information stored in computers.

Mainframe—The central processing unit (CPU), power supply, and other components permanently connected to the CPU.

Matrix—A data structure similar to an array except that it is multi-dimensional. Each data element is specified by its numeric position in the columns and rows.

Megahertz—Millions of cycles (usually of a clock) per second.

Memory-addressing modes—The ways in which memory addresses are specified in memory move instructions.

Microfiche—A card format microform containing as many as 400 pages on a single piece of film.

Microform—A reduced size image containing information that can be read by humans only after magnification. Microfilm and microfiche are two types of microform.

Microprogramming section—The section of a central processing unit (CPU) that encodes instructions into specific actions of the registers, arithmetic and logic unit (ALU), and internal bus.

Millions of instructions per second—A number related to the rate at which a central processing unit (CPU) can carry out instructions.

Minuend—In subtraction, the number from which the subtrahend is subtracted.

MIPS—*See* millions of instructions per second.

Mnemonic—An abbreviated name given to an instruction to aid assembly level programmers in writing programs. Assembler programs can convert these names into the object codes that a given computer can understand.

Appendix A 157

Modem—Modulator/demodulator, a device that converts digital information from a computer into a communication signal and vice versa.

Modular programming—A programming technique that divides the problem into subparts to make the solution more manageable. This is similar to structured programming.

Monitor—A program that handles low-level tasks associated with instructing computers. Usually, this includes a bootstrap program and programs to handle file management. Sometimes, more elaborate monitors are called operating systems.

Most significant bit—*See* significance.

Multiprogramming—Computer programming that allows several users to run programs simultaneously on the same computer.

Nesting—Calling a subroutine from within a subroutine.

Object codes—Binary codes that the microprogramming section of a central processing unit (CPU) can interpret.

OCR—*See* optical character recognition.

Octal numbers—Numbers written in base 8, which correspond to all the possible permutations of three bits.

On-line—Computer systems that perform programs immediately after the command is given.

Operating system—An elaborate monitor program that handles system-wide commands to the computer. It may include programming to allow multiple simultaneous usage.

Operator—A mathematical symbol that defines a specific process to be performed on operands placed in appropriate positions relative to the operator.

Optical character recognition—A form of computer input in which a machine reads printed characters.

Page-directed addressing—A memory-addressing mode in which the high-order byte of the referenced address is fixed by the system design and the low-order byte is given immediately following the instruction.

Parallel communication—Communication that proceeds a byte at a time.

Parity—A mechanism for checking the integrity of a communication channel. When defined as even, there must be an even number of bits in the data stream; when odd, an odd number of bits.

PC register—*See* program counter.

Plotter—A device that draws pictures under control of a computer.

Pop—*See* pull.

Position—*See* significance.

Power on jump—The first instruction a computer performs when the power is turned on. It causes the computer to start performing instructions placed at a specified location in memory.

Precedence rules—Rules in a language that define the order in which mathematical operations in complex commands are performed.

Programmable read only memory—Memory, usually composed of semiconductor circuits, that is relatively easy to program after manufacture and is usually also randomly accessible.

Program counter—The part of a computer that stores the address of the next instruction to be performed.

PROM—*See* programmable read only memory.

Pull—The process of decreasing the stack pointer once or twice and moving the information on the stack to a register in the central processing unit (CPU).

Push—The process of placing information at the top of the stack and changing the stack pointer to reflect the new top of the stack.

Quotient—The result of division.

Radio frequency modulator—A device that converts a composite video output signal into a radio frequency signal that can be picked up and displayed by an unmodified television set.

RAM—*See* random access memory.

Random access memory—Memory that may be accessed in random sequence. This term is commonly used to indicate read/write (R/W) memory (memory which can be read from or written to). Semiconductor circuits are usually used to build it.

Read only memory—Memory, usually composed of semiconductor circuits, that may not be written to after manufacture. Access may be random. Sometimes this term is used to indicate programmable or erasable types of read only memory.

Realtime—Computer systems that perform programs immediately after the command is given.

Record—A data structure, usually of a fixed size, that contains information about given entities in fields. Records are usually assembled into a file with a fixed structure.

Registers—Special memory areas of a central processing unit (CPU) that contain data to be manipulated and their results.

RF modulator—*See* radio frequency modulator.

ROM—*See* read only memory.

RS232—A standard for connecting serial communication devices, that defines the function and position of several wires, handshaking signals to be used, and electrical characteristics of data transmitted.

R/W memory—*See* random access memory.

Serial communication—Communication that proceeds a bit at a time.

Significance—The significance or position of a digit that determines the interpretation of the digit's value. The least significant digit is the rightmost digit, and the most significant digit is the leftmost digit. The position of the digit is given by counting toward the left from the decimal point, beginning at 0. The interpretation is that the base raised to position equals the value. Positions counted to the right from the decimal point are given a minus sign, and their interpretation is the same—the digit times the value of the base raised to the power of the position.

Software—Computer programs.

SP—*See* stack pointer.

Stack—An area of memory reserved for storing addresses of program code when subroutines are called. When a return is executed, these addresses are loaded back into the program counter. A stack is also sometimes used to store data temporarily during programs.

Stack pointer—A register that contains the least significant byte of the address of the stack.

Static random access memory (RAM)—RAM that does not lose its contents as long as power is connected.

String—A variable composed of alphabetic or numeric characters that are never manipulated mathematically.

Structured programming—A programming style that involves dividing the program into smaller parts and reassembling them into a fixed format of parts.

Subtrahend—In subtraction, the number being subtracted from the minuend.

Synchronous circuits—Electronic circuits that produce their result only after a specific clock signal is received. These circuits form the basis of computer memory, shift, and move operations.

Synchronous serial communication—A mode of serial communication in which data are constantly transmitted at the specified speed. Synch characters are used to fill in spaces when no data are available.

Syntax—The exact spelling, punctuation, and organization of commands required in a computer language.

System bus—A set of data paths that connect the central processing unit (CPU) with the rest of the computer.

System clock—*See* clock.

Systems analysis—The process of determining the algorithm for the solution of a complex problem.

Tens complement—The number that, when added to a given number, gives 10. *See* complement.

Time-sharing—Use of a multiprogrammed computer.

Track—A concentric circle on a disk in which information is stored.

Transistor—An electronic device that functions like an electrically controllable switch. Transistors form the basic circuits that make up computers.

Truth table—A table that gives for each possible value of the inputs, the correct outputs for a given operator.

Twos complement—The number that, when added to a given number, gives 2. *See* complement.

Unary operator—NOT; also, nonoperator NO CHANGE.

Variable—A data structure in which a varying numeric or string value is assigned to a mnemonic.

Video digitizers—Electronic circuits that convert the output of a video camera into digital information that can be processed by a computer.

Volatile memory—Memory that is erased when power is turned off.

Word size—In a computer, the number of bits that are processed simultaneously.

# Appendix B
ASCII and EBCDIC Codes

appendix B

Decimal	Hexadecimal	Binary	ASCII Character	EBCDIC Character
00	00	0000 0000	NUL	NUL
01	01	0000 0001	SOH	SOH
02	02	0000 0010	STX	STX
03	03	0000 0011	ETX	ETX
04	04	0000 0100	EOT	
05	05	0000 0101	ENQ	HT
06	06	0000 0110	ACK	
07	07	0000 0111	BEL	DEL
08	08	0000 1000	BS	
09	09	0000 1001	HT	
10	0A	0000 1010	LF	
11	0B	0000 1011	VT	VT
12	0C	0000 1100	FF	FF
13	0D	0000 1101	CR	CR
14	0E	0000 1110	SO	SO
15	0F	0000 1111	SI	SI
16	10	0001 0000	DLE	DLE
17	11	0001 0001	DC1	DC1
18	12	0001 0010	DC2	DC2
19	13	0001 0011	DC3	DC3
20	14	0001 0100	DC4	
21	15	0001 0101	NAK	
22	16	0001 0110	SYN	BS
23	17	0001 0111	ETB	
24	18	0001 1000	CAN	CAN

Decimal	Hexadecimal	Binary	ASCII Character	EBCDIC Character
25	19	0001 1001	EM	EM
26	1A	0001 1010	SUB	
27	1B	0001 1011	ESC	
28	1C	0001 1100	FS	FS
29	1D	0001 1101	GS	GS
30	1E	0001 1110	BS	RS
31	1F	0001 1111	US	US
32	20	0010 0000	BLANK	
33	21	0010 0001	!	
34	22	0010 0010	"	
35	23	0010 0011	#	
36	24	0010 0100	$	
37	25	0010 0101	%	LF
38	26	0010 0110	@	ETB
39	27	0010 0111	'	ESC
40	28	0010 1000	(	
41	29	0010 1001	)	
42	2A	0010 1010	*	
43	2B	0010 1011	+	
44	2C	0010 1100	,	
45	2D	0010 1101	-	ENQ
46	2E	0010 1110		ACK
47	2F	0010 1111	/	BEL
48	30	0011 0000	0	
49	31	0011 0001	1	
50	32	0011 0010	2	SYN
51	33	0011 0011	3	
52	34	0011 0100	4	
53	35	0011 0101	5	
54	36	0011 0110	6	
55	37	0011 0111	7	
56	38	0011 1000	8	
57	39	0011 1001	9	
58	3A	0011 1010	:	
59	3B	0011 1011	;	
60	3C	0011 1100		DC4
61	3D	0011 1101	=	NAK
62	3E	0011 1110		

Appendix B   165

Decimal	Hexadecimal	Binary	ASCII Character	EBCDIC Character
63	3F	0011 1111	?	SUB
64	40	0100 0000	@	SPACE
65	41	0100 0001	A	
66	42	0100 0010	B	
67	43	0100 0011	C	
68	44	0100 0100	D	
69	45	0100 0101	E	
70	46	0100 0110	F	
71	47	0100 0111	G	
72	48	0100 1000	H	
73	49	0100 1001	I	
74	4A	0100 1010	J	[
75	4B	0100 1011	K	.
76	4C	0100 1100	L	<
77	4D	0100 1101	M	(
78	4E	0100 1110	N	+
79	4F	0100 1111	O	!
80	50	0101 0000	P	&
81	51	0101 0001	Q	
82	52	0101 0010	R	
83	53	0101 0011	S	
84	54	0101 0100	T	
85	55	0101 0101	U	
86	56	0101 0110	V	
87	57	0101 0111	W	
88	58	0101 1000	X	
89	59	0101 1001	Y	
90	5A	0101 1010	Z	]
91	5B	0101 1011		$
92	5C	0101 1100		*
93	5D	0101 1101		)
94	5E	0101 1110		;
95	5F	0101 1111		^
96	60	0110 0000		-
97	61	0110 0001	a	/
98	62	0110 0010	b	
99	63	0110 0011	c	
100	64	0110 0100	d	

Decimal	Hexadecimal	Binary	ASCII Character	EBCDIC Character
101	65	0110 0101	e	
102	66	0110 0110	f	
103	67	0110 0111	g	
104	68	0110 1000	h	
105	69	0110 1001	i	
106	6A	0110 1010	j	|
107	6B	0110 1011	k	,
108	6C	0110 1100	l	%
109	6D	0110 1101	m	_
110	6E	0110 1110	n	>
111	6F	0110 1111	o	?
112	70	0111 0000	p	
113	71	0111 0001	q	
114	72	0111 0010	r	
115	73	0111 0011	s	
116	74	0111 0100	t	
117	75	0111 0101	u	
118	76	0111 0110	v	
119	77	0111 0111	w	
120	78	0111 1000	x	
121	79	0111 1001	y	
122	7A	0111 1010	z	:
123	7B	0111 1011		#
124	7C	0111 1100		@
125	7D	0111 1101		'
126	7E	0111 1110		=
127	7F	0111 1111		"
128	80	1000 0000		
129	81	1000 0001		a
130	82	1000 0010		b
131	83	1000 0011		c
132	84	1000 0100		d
133	85	1000 0101		e
134	86	1000 0110		f
135	87	1000 0111		g
136	88	1000 1000		h
137	89	1000 1001		i
138	8A	1000 1010		

Appendix B 167

Decimal	Hexadecimal	Binary	ASCII Character	EBCDIC Character
139	8B	1000 1011		
140	8C	1000 1100		
141	8D	1000 1101		
142	8E	1000 1110		
143	8F	1000 1111		
144	90	1001 0000		
145	91	1001 0001		j
146	92	1001 0010		k
147	93	1001 0011		l
148	94	1001 0100		m
149	95	1001 0101		n
150	96	1001 0110		o
151	97	1001 0111		p
152	98	1001 1000		q
153	99	1001 1001		r
154	9A	1001 1010		
155	9B	1001 1011		
156	9C	1001 1100		
157	9D	1001 1101		
158	9E	1001 1110		
159	9F	1001 1111		
160	A0	1010 0000		
161	A1	1010 0001		
162	A2	1010 0010		s
163	A3	1010 0011		t
164	A4	1010 0100		u
165	A5	1010 0101		v
166	A6	1010 0110		w
167	A7	1010 0111		x
168	A8	1010 1000		y
169	A9	1010 1001		z
170	AA	1010 1010		
171	AB	1010 1011		
172	AC	1010 1100		
173	AD	1010 1101		
174	AE	1010 1110		
175	AF	1010 1111		
176	B0	1011 0000		

Decimal	Hexadecimal	Binary	ASCII Character	EBCDIC Character
177	B1	1011 0001		
178	B2	1011 0010		
179	B3	1011 0011		
180	B4	1011 0100		
181	B5	1011 0101		
182	B6	1011 0110		
183	B7	1011 0111		
184	B8	1011 1000		
185	B9	1011 1001		
186	BA	1011 1010		
187	BB	1011 1011		
188	BC	1011 1100		
189	BD	1011 1101		
190	BE	1011 1110		
191	BF	1011 1111		
192	C0	1100 0000		{
193	C1	1100 0001		A
194	C2	1100 0010		B
195	C3	1100 0011		C
196	C4	1100 0100		D
197	C5	1100 0101		E
198	C6	1100 0110		F
199	C7	1100 0111		G
200	C8	1100 1000		H
201	C9	1100 1001		I
202	CA	1100 1010		
203	CB	1100 1011		
204	CC	1100 1100		
205	CD	1100 1101		
206	CE	1100 1110		
207	CF	1100 1111		
208	D0	1101 0000		}
209	D1	1101 0001		J
210	D2	1101 0010		K
211	D3	1101 0011		L
212	D4	1101 0100		M
213	D5	1101 0101		N

Appendix B

Decimal	Hexadecimal	Binary	ASCII Character	EBCDIC Character
214	D6	1101 0110		O
215	D7	1101 0111		P
216	D8	1101 1000		Q
217	D9	1101 1001		R
218	DA	1101 1010		
219	DB	1101 1011		
220	DC	1101 1100		
221	DD	1101 1101		
222	DE	1101 1110		
223	DF	1101 1111		
224	E0	1110 0000		\
225	E1	1110 0001		
226	E2	1110 0010		S
227	E3	1110 0011		T
228	E4	1110 0100		U
229	E5	1110 0101		V
230	E6	1110 0110		W
231	E7	1110 0111		X
232	E8	1110 1000		Y
233	E9	1110 1001		Z
234	EA	1110 1010		
235	EB	1110 1011		
236	EC	1110 1100		
237	ED	1110 1101		
238	EE	1110 1110		
239	EF	1110 1111		
240	F0	1111 0000		0
241	F1	1111 0001		1
242	F2	1111 0010		2
243	F3	1111 0011		3
244	F4	1111 0100		4
245	F5	1111 0101		5
246	F6	1111 0110		6
247	F7	1111 0111		7
248	F8	1111 1000		8
249	F9	1111 1001		
250	FA	1111 1010		

Decimal	Hexadecimal	Binary	ASCII Character	EBCDIC Character
251	FB	1111 1011		
252	FC	1111 1100		
253	FD	1111 1101		
254	FE	1111 1110		
255	FF	1111 1111		

Appendix C
Sample BASIC Program

appendix C

```
100 DIM L (100),R(100),K$(100)
200 PRINT "SELECT ONE BY NUMBER:"
210 PRINT "1. CREATE TREE"
220 PRINT "2. SORT AND LIST TREE"
230 PRINT "3. STOP"
240 INPUT A
250 ON A GOTO 300,500,10000
300 PRINT "HOW MANY ENTRIES?"
310 INPUT T
320 FOR N=1 TO T
330 PRINT "ENTER KEY VALUE"
340 INPUT K$(N)
350 NEXT N
360 GOSUB 900
370 GOTO 200
500 GOSUB 1230
510 GOTO 200
900 F=0
910 T1=1
920 N1=0
990 FOR N=1 TO T
1000 E=F
1010 R=1
1020 P=R
1030 I=F
1040 IF K$(N)<=K$(P) THEN 1130
1050 IF R(P)<=0 THEN 1080
1060 P=R(P)
1070 GOTO 1200
1080 R(N)=R(P)
```

```
1090 R(P)=N
1100 L(N)=N1
1110 I=T
1120 GOTO 1200
1130 IF L(P)<>N1 THEN 1190
1140 L(P)=N
1150 L(N)=N1
1160 R(N)=-P
1170 I=T
1180 GOTO 1200
1190 P=L(P)
1200 IF I=F THEN 1040
1210 NEXT N
1215 RETURN
1220 REM SORT STARTS HERE
1230 P=R
1240 F1=F
1250 IF L(P)=N1 THEN 1280
1260 P=L(P)
1270 GOTO 1250
1280 IF ((R(P)<>N1) AND (F1=F)) THEN 1300
1290 GOTO 1360
1300 PRINT K$(P)
1310 GOSUB 1390
1320 P=S
1330 IF P<>N1 THEN 1280
1340 F1=T1
1350 GOTO 1280
1360 IF F1<>F THEN 1380
1370 PRINT K$(P)
1380 RETURN
1390 Q=R(P)
1400 IF R(P)>N1 THEN 1430
1410 Q=-Q
1415 PRINT "Q=",Q
1420 GOTO 1460
1430 IF L(Q)=0 THEN 1460
1440 Q=L(Q)
1450 GOTO 1430
1460 S=Q
1470 RETURN
10000 END
```

Appendix D
Sample Pascal Program

appendix D

```
Program Tree (input, output);
Type
nodeptr                    =   ^nde;
nde                        =   record
    left                   :   nodeptr;
    right                  :   nodeptr;
    key                    :   string;
end; {nde}

Var

tempkey                    :   string;
selection, ans             :   char;
root, treepoint,
nodepoint                  :   nodeptr;
insert, stop               :   boolean;

procedure maketree;

begin
writeln ('enter key value or press return');
readln (tempkey);
insert : = false;
new (nodepoint);
nodepoint^.left: = nil;
nodepoint^.right: = nil;
nodepoint^.key : = tempkey;
```

```
treepoint: = root;
repeat {until insert}

if root^.key = ""
   then
      begin
         root^.key : = tempkey;
         insert : = true
      end
   else
    if tempkey < treepoint^.key
    then
       if treepoint^.left = nil
          then
          begin
             treepoint^.left : = nodepoint;
             insert : = true
          end
          else
          treepoint : = treepoint^.left
    else
       if treepoint^.right = nil
          then
          begin
             treepoint^.right : = nodepoint;
             insert : = true
          end
          else
          treepoint : = treepoint^.right
until insert
end; {maketree}

Procedure list (var p:nodeptr);
```

```
begin
    if p<>nil then
        begin
                list (p^.left);
                writeln (p^.key);
                list (p^.right)
        end
end; {list}

begin
new (root);
root^.left: = nil;
root^.right: = nil;
root^.key := "";
stop: = false;

repeat
    writeln ('select one');
    writeln ('(E)nter string');
    writeln ('(L)ist inorder');
    writeln ('(S)top');
    read (selection);
    writeln;

    case selection of
            'E','e' :  repeat

                            maketree;

                       until tempkey = "";

            'L','l' :  list (root);

            'S','s' :  stop := true;

    end; {case}
until stop;

end. {tree}
```

Appendix E
Sample Proposal To Conduct Systems Analysis

appendix E

DATE:

TO: Hospital Administration

FROM: Pharmacy Systems Team

SUBJECT: Pharmacy Systems Analysis

PROBLEM DEFINITION

The management of the pharmacy department wishes to perform general systems improvements; specifically, it desires to take advantage of the capabilities of computers to increase departmental productivity and to improve management control. This document presents a proposal to perform general systems analysis in order to gather information that will allow redesign of such systems or subsystems as the management desires.

The estimated time to perform this analysis is approximately 1,200 personnel hours. At current salary levels, this represents a cost of approximately $20,000.00 including fringe benefits and overhead.

If this proposal is accepted, the systems group will complete the analysis and present a full report to the management. Included in that report will be an estimate of redesign costs for each subsystem and system in the department.

The remainder of this proposal is organized as follows:

1. anticipated benefits of the analysis
2. preliminary observed requirements and constraints
3. scope of proposed analyses
4. facts and sources needed
5. potential problems

6. explanation of personnel requirements
7. anticipated contents of Systems Analyses Completion Report

ANTICIPATED BENEFITS OF A GENERAL SYSTEMS ANALYSIS

In performing a general systems analysis, the systems team will examine every significant individual repetitive action performed by the staff and will analyze its efficiency, its interaction with other activities, and its contribution to departmental goals. The ways in which the pharmacy department, as a whole, operates and the ways in which it interacts with other hospital departments will also be determined. The analyses will give the design team a complete, clear picture of departmental operation. The team can then design an effective new system as desired by the management.

The advantage of a general systems analysis rather than a specific systems analysis is that the general analysis provides information about subsystem and macrosystem interactions, thus making it possible to increase the efficiency of these interactions. It also provides information useful in making decisions concerning the optimal order of implementation of subsystems. A specific subsystem analysis has only a single advantage: it is faster.

The benefits of analysis are expected to include the following:

- The design phase should be more efficient and less costly than if performed without analysis.
- The design features should be more effective than if created without an analysis.
- The analysis document itself should provide a useful management tool.
- The flow of information between subdepartments and with other departments should be more efficient than if design is performed without an analysis.
- The implementation of new systems and subsystems within or outside of the department should proceed with fewer obstacles than without an analysis.
- A general systems analysis will reduce the risk of creating an excessively costly or ineffective computer system.

PERFORMANCE REQUIREMENTS AND CONSTRAINTS

Subsystems

1. Backup system
2. Admissions, discharge, and transfer (ADT)

3. Inventory and ordering
4. Fill lists and labels
5. IV labels and IV fill list/worklist
6. Drug utilization reports
7. Automatic reorder and station stock
8. Patient billing
9. Formulary master drug list
10. Group purchasing system
11. Drug-drug interactions, laboratory interaction, allergy monitoring
12. Narcotic control
13. Extemporaneous compounding
14. Drug information retrieval
15. Record of medication administration to patients
16. Budget preparation

Subsystem Information Requirements and Sources

1. Patient profile
   a. patient name: ADT, hospital census
   b. room number and station: ADT
   c. drug name: physician order form
   d. drug dose: physician order form
   e. drug dosage form: physician order form
   f. frequency or time: physician order form
   g. allergies: medical record
   h. diagnosis: medical record
2. Admission, discharge, and transfer
   a. patient room and station number: patient admitting
   b. date of entry into the hospital: patient admitting
   c. birthdate: patient admitting
   d. past allergies: patient admitting or pharmacist interview
3. Inventory and ordering
   a. drug name, form, package size: formulary or drug list subsystem
   b. economical reorder point: past experience
   c. current inventory: orders received, transactions
   d. amount on order: ordering data, hospital purchasing
   e. monthly, yearly utilization by physician, station, unit transactions
4. IV labels and IV worklist
   a. patient name, station number, room number: ADT
   b. drugs, cost: physician order form
   c. discontinue orders: nurse's notes or physician order form
   d. amount and rate administered: nurse's notes or input/output sheets

e. concentration available, concentration desired, how to make: master drug list
5. Drug utilization reports
   a. criteria and standards: committee
   b. patient data: medical record/laboratory record
   c. amounts of drug used (e.g., by station, physician) and other factors: transaction data
6. Automatic reorder system (Noncharge floor stock)
   a. list of drugs on system: administrator's decision
   b. label generation information: fixed format
   c. nurse's station stock: routine inventory by pharmacy personnel
7. Patient billing
   a. patient name: ADT
   b. drug name, size, product type: transaction data
   c. item unit price: drug list, formulary system
   d. number units received: transaction data
   e. date of drug administration
8. Formulary or master drug list
   a. drug names, status: pharmacy and therapeutics committee
   b. product descriptions: pharmacy and therapeutics committee, pharmacy decision
   c. cost, price: purchasing agent, bid system
9. Group purchasing
   a. supplier's address: address list
   b. formulary list of items to be stocked: formulary system
   c. estimated yearly utilization: inventory system/profile system
   d. contract forms: hospital legal department
10. Drug interactions, laboratory drug allergy
    a. list of drugs causing interactions: literature
    b. patient data: profile system
    c. supporting drug literature for pharmacy staff use: literature
11. Narcotic control
    a. drug name: profile or control sheet, master drug list
    b. person administering: nursing personnel, administration profile
    c. amount wasted, if any: nursing personnel
    d. charge, if any: master drug list
    e. patient name: profile
    f. current station inventory before administering: nursing personnel or eight-hour inventories
    g. current station inventory after administering: nursing personnel
    h. unique item number of the unit administered to patient: profile
    i. physician ordering: medical record or nursing personnel

j. time of administration: nursing personnel or profile
12. Extemporaneous compounding
    a. product name or description: pharmacist who made it first
    b. ingredients and amounts: pharmacist who made it first
    c. procedure: pharmacist, literature
    d. labeling: pharmacist, law, experience
    e. stability data and compatibility: pharmacist, drug list
    f. source of information: drug literature
13. Drug information retrieval
    a. miscellaneous data bases (e.g., international pharmaceutical abstracts)
14. Nonstock drug request
    a. reason for request: physician order form
    b. product description: pharmacist
    c. physician name: physician order form
    d. decision to add to formulary: physician
    e. cost: pharmacist, drug information system
    f. date ordered/received by pharmacist: inventory system
    g. amount ordered: pharmacist, purchasing system
    h. form completed: pharmacist, physician
15. Special reports
    a. budget assistance (e.g., overtime hours by month for previous year)
    b. scheduling system
        1) employee name
        2) employment type (e.g., part-time)
        3) dates of vacation, leave requested
        4) allotment of requests available (e.g., sick leave, leave of absence, weekends)
        5) date and hours scheduled to work
        6) dates of leave taken
        7) overtime hours, holidays, vacations worked
    c. resource monitoring
        1) activity codes for employee's activities, employee name, position, status
        2) spot checks on employee activities
        3) supervisory personnel achievement reports (monthly)
16. System utilities
    a. data base management system
    b. word processing

Subsystem Interdependency Analysis Based on Information Flow, Not Departmental Operation

1. Patient profile
   a. requirements
      1) creation of or interface with ADT
      2) existing physician order form system
      3) interface with medical records of allergy, diagnosis problem list
   b. essential to (highly)
      1) inventory system
      2) patient billing
2. Admission, discharge, and transfer
   a. requirement: good interface with pharmacy
   b. essential to (very high)
      1) patient profile
      2) IV labels
      3) patient billing
   c. essential to (indirectly) inventory
3. inventory and ordering
   a. requirements
      1) profile system, unless based on shelf observation
      2) formulary or drug list system
      3) hospital purchasing interface
   b. essential
4. IV system
   a. requirements
      1) ADT
      2) order form collection system
      3) nursing information interface
      4) formulary
   b. essential to (low) drug interactions/allergy system
5. Drug utilization reports
   a. requirements
      1) criteria and standards
      2) medical record readers
      3) profile transaction data
   b. unused by other systems
6. Noncharge floor stock
   a. requirements
      1) list of items
      2) inventory by pharmacy personnel

b. essential to (low) inventory system
7. Patient billing
   a. requirements
      1) ADT
      2) profile system
      3) formulary
   b. unused by other systems
8. Formulary, master drug list
   a. requirements
      1) pharmacy and therapeutics committee
      2) nonstock system
      3) medical staff policy
      4) inventory and ordering
      5) bid
   b. essential to (high)
      1) patient billing
      2) patient profile
      3) inventory and ordering
      4) IV labels
   c. essential to (indirectly)
      1) drug utilization report
      2) noncharge floor stock, bid
      3) drug interactions
      4) narcotic control
      5) nonstock drug request
      6) budget and management reports
9. Bid system
   a. requirements
      1) suppliers list
      2) master drug list
      3) inventory
      4) hospital legal department
   b. essential to (indirectly)
      1) formulary
      2) patient billing
      3) patient profiles
10. Drug interactions
    a. requirements
       1) drug literature
       2) capture (in machine-readable form)
       3) profile (manual equivalent of patient clinical information)
    b. unused by other systems

11. Narcotic control
    a. requirements
       1) master drug list
       2) patient profile order input system
       3) nursing capture
    b. unused by other systems
12. Extemporaneous compounding
    a. requirements
       1) drug literature
       2) training and experience of pharmacist
    b. unused by other systems
13. Drug information retrieval
    a. requirements: stands alone
    b. essential to
       1) drug interactions/allergy
       2) formulary
       3) extemporaneous compounding
14. Nonformulary drug requests
    a. requirements
       1) formulary
       2) drug information
       3) inventory and ordering
    b. essential to formulary
15. Special reports
    a. requirements
       1) employee data capture
       2) activity codes
    b. totally optional but a time saver, political power builder
16. System utilities
    a. requirements: only a piece of hardware with software
    b. time saver only

Constraints

1. System must interface with existing patient billing system, both hardware and software.
2. Manual backup must be designed, and it must be possible to implement backup instantly.
3. System must provide patient confidentiality.
4. System must be secure.
5. System must provide accurate financial information.

6. System must provide accurate patient information.
7. System must abide by all pertinent laws.

SCOPE OF ANALYSIS

The proposed analysis is to center on the pharmacy department's operation. All subsystems and significant activities of the pharmacy department will be analyzed. Whenever information is obtained from or sent to other departments, its source, content, and format will be identified. Also, special media or forms used in extradepartmental communication will be documented.

All vended commercial hospital pharmacy systems will be analyzed via request for proposal. Vendors will be identified as those who advertise at the next American Society of Hospital Pharmacists Midyear Clinical Meeting. If follow-up questions are appropriate, they will be pursued.

Two or three local (in state) hospital pharmacy computer systems will be cursorily analyzed by means of one-day on-site interviews with management and systems staff.

FACTS AND SOURCES NEEDED

Facts

1. Organizational chart and job descriptions
2. Current configuration and data processing methods
3. General statistical information concerning current system
    a. number of inpatient days per year
    b. number of unit doses dispensed per time period and range
    c. number of outpatient prescriptions filled per unit time
4. Specific information needs identified by anticipated major users
5. All forms used inside and outside department

Sources

1. Interviews with all pharmacy
2. Existing policy and procedure manuals
3. Interviews with systems personnel from within hospital
4. Interviews with personnel (e.g., nurses, respiratory therapists) who interact with pharmacy services on a routine basis
5. Proposals from vendors

6. Interviews with management and systems personnel from other local hospitals

POTENTIAL PROBLEMS

1. Patient confidentiality legislation
2. Internal control of a system handling large numbers of transactions and moderately large sums of money
3. Interfacing with existing hospital data processing procedures
4. Interfacing of hardware with existing hospital hardware
5. Interfacing with existing management procedures
6. Federal, state, and local regulations mandating such things as patient package inserts, profit reporting, and performance monitoring
7. Line voltage fluctuations affecting hardware performance
8. System reliability

PERSONNEL

Research	400 hours
Interviewing	200 hours
Analyzing facts	400 hours
Compiling and preparing report	200 hours
Communicating findings	16 hours
Total	1,216 hours

ANTICIPATED CONTENTS OF ANALYSIS REPORT

The analysis report will contain the following:

1. Summary of findings and explanations
2. Information flowcharts
   a. between pharmacy and other hospital systems
   b. within and between subsystems
3. Hardware requirements and constraints
4. Software requirements and constraints
5. Recommended system controls
6. Conclusions
7. Appendixes
   a. tables of findings
   b. estimated design costs

Appendix F
Systems Analyses Completion Report

appendix F

A full-fledged systems analyses completion report takes a good year to produce and is specific to one particular system. The contents of such a report are described in the following.

OPERATIONAL SYSTEM

The purpose of the section on the operational system is to describe fully the system currently installed in the hospital under study. It should include descriptions of

1. the operational system. This section is an overview of what the system does and how; it does not contain an action-by-action description. The details of every action are portrayed on the flowcharts in the appendixes.
2. interfaces. The way in which the pharmacy system interfaces with other hospital and outside world systems is described in some detail. The interaction among subsystems within the existing pharmacy system is also described.
3. controls. In this section, control of the existing system is described. Current feedback available to the managers and staff are outlined in some detail. Information used to control the system is described.
4. decision points. Tactical, strategic, and operational decisions made in the day-to-day operation of the existing system are outlined. The information needed for these decisions is detailed.
5. transaction processing procedures. A prose description of the flowcharts, highlighting information needed for transactions, is presented in this section.

ALTERNATIVE SYSTEMS ANALYSES

The operational system analysis is applied to the systems visited and those documented through information obtained in the request for proposal process in the section on alternative systems analyses. The requests for proposal, as well as responses to them, are included in the appendixes.

QUANTITATIVE DATA

A prose summary of the data collected regarding quantitative aspects of the existing system is included. This tells how often the actions documented in the analysis section appear to be performed. The implications of this for machine selection are explained. Additional constraints in the software are also explained. The actual data collected are presented in the appendixes.

OBJECTIVES STATEMENTS

The objectives as stated throughout the many iterations of the objective setting process are documented. Emphasis is on the current set of objectives statements.

PROPOSAL TO INITIATE DESIGN EFFORT

If the decision is to design a new system, a proposal to initiate a design effort must be included. A similar, but less lengthy proposal would be included if the decision is to use a particular vended system. The proposal should include

1. rationale. A short justification for the decision to go with a design effort is presented. By this point, the data to support such a decision should have been provided.
2. cost estimation. An accurate estimation of the cost of the entire development effort is included. This should include costs of personnel, equipment, supplies, and any space renovation. It is usually wise to make estimates on the high side because it may be difficult to ask for more money later to complete the project and because inflation and unforeseen costs may increase the amount required. This approach makes approval harder to obtain, but results in a greater chance for long-term success of the project.

3. plan for proceeding. An overview of the plan for proceeding if the proposal is accepted is presented. The exact plan is detailed in the form of a PERT chart, Gantt chart, or some other planning device in the appendixes. This section gives the major checkpoints in the plan.
4. implications of denial. The likely implications if the proposal is not accepted must be discussed.

APPENDIXES

The appendixes should include

1. flowcharts
2. quantitative operational system data
3. sample request for proposal
4. responses to the request for proposal
5. comparison charts of alternative systems
6. PERT or other planning document

Appendix G
A Quick Review of Number Systems

appendix G

A number system can be defined as a system for adding (counting), subtracting, multiplying, and dividing. Two attributes of number systems are (1) procedures for these operations and (2) numerals to represent numbers. It has been seen that the procedures for performing these operations in binary are really the same as those in the decimal system, but that since binary systems have only two numerals to deal with, some shortcuts can be taken.

Numbers are abstract concepts of the human mind. Humans seem to be born with a sense of bigger or smaller, greater or lesser, and an instinct to quantitate and enumerate these differences. The human mind usually has difficulty dealing quantitatively with abstractions, however, which is why numerals were invented. Numerals are graphic designs that are used to represent numbers. Examples of numerals are the familiar Arabic (1, 2, 3, 4, . . .) and the archaic Roman (I, II, III, IV, . . .).

The number system that is used almost exclusively in trade and commerce in the Western world is the Arabic-decimal system, i.e., a base 10 system that uses Arabic numerals. The base of a number system is the number that determines the interpretation of the position of a numeral within a number. Thus, in the number 345, the meaning of the 3 is greater than the meaning of the 5, owing to its position in the number. This is because the third position to the left of the decimal point, referred to as the most significant digit, is the hundreds position. The second position is the tens position, and the first position is the ones position. This relationship can be generalized by saying that the interpretation of the value of a position is equal to the base of the number system raised to the power of the ordinate of that position, counting from right to left, minus 1. Thus, the number 12,345.0 is literally:

$$(1 \times 10^{5-1}) + (2 \times 10^{4-1}) + (3 \times 10^{3-1}) + (4 \times 10^{2-1}) + (5 \times 10^{1-1})$$

in the base 10 system. Positions are sometimes given the number that corresponds to the power of the base that they represent. Thus, the position immediately to the left of the decimal point, called the least significant digit, is position 0. The one to its left is position 1, and so on. This numbering system is the source of much confusion, since humans have a tendency to start numbering at 1, not 0.

Remember that any number raised to the 0 power is, by definition, equal to 1, and any number raised to the power of 1 is that number. A common way of indicating the base of a number, if there is any possibility of confusion, is to write the base as a subscript after the number; for example, $12,345_{10}$.

If a number is to be changed from one base to another, the value that 1 would have in the new base is calculated in each position, the number in each position is multiplied by the appropriate number thus derived, and the numbers thus obtained are added. For example, to convert 1312_4 (in base 4) to its decimal (base 10) equivalent,

```
Values of positions
  first position   1 × 4^(1-1) = 1 × 4^0 = 1 × 1 = 1
  second position  1 × 4^(2-1) = 1 × 4^1         = 4
  third position   1 × 4^(3-1) = 1 × 4^2         = 16
  fourth position  1 × 4^(4-1) = 1 × 4^3         = 64
```

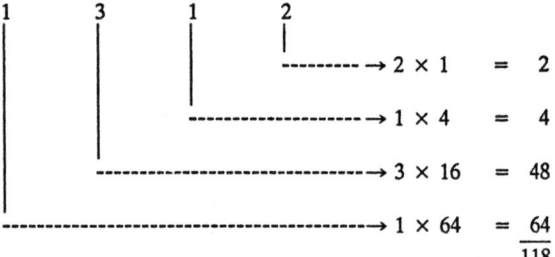

$$
\begin{array}{rcl}
2 \times 1 & = & 2 \\
1 \times 4 & = & 4 \\
3 \times 16 & = & 48 \\
1 \times 64 & = & 64 \\
\hline
& & 118
\end{array}
$$

The answer is $1312_4 = 118_{10}$.

Changing from decimal to another base is a little more difficult. This can be done by starting in the position next to the decimal point and calculating the values a 1 would have in each position, until the value of a given position is greater than that of the decimal number being converted.

When this is found, the decimal number is divided by the position value of the next lowest position. The single digit whole number result is the value that belongs in that position of the new base number. The remainder is then divided by the value of the next lowest position, and so on, until the decimal point is reached. For example, if the base 5 value of the decimal number 894 was needed, the position values would be calculated as follows:

$$\text{position 1: } 5^0 = 1$$
$$\text{position 2: } 5^1 = 5$$
$$\text{position 3: } 5^2 = 25$$
$$\text{position 4: } 5^3 = 125$$
$$\text{position 5: } 5^4 = 625$$
$$\text{position 6: } 5^5 = 3125$$

Calculation is stopped at position 6 because it is the first position that has a value greater than 894_{10}. The next step is to divide 894 by 625, the next lowest value. The result is 1. Thus, position 5 will hold 1.

5	4	3	2	1
1	?	?	?	?

The remainder is 269. Then, 269 is divided by 125, giving 2, the number in the fourth position.

5	4	3	2	1
1	2	?	?	?

The remainder is 19. Ordinarily, this number would be divided by 25, but 19 is less than 25. Thus, a 0 is placed in position 3.

5	4	3	2	1
1	2	0	?	?

The remainder is still 19. Dividing 19 by 5 gives 3, which is the number in the second position.

5	4	3	2	1
1	2	0	3	?

The remainder is 4. Then, 4 is divided by 1. The result is 4, with no remainder. The number in the first position is 4. There is never a remainder after this position unless a decimal point was used.

5	4	3	2	1
1	2	0	3	4

Thus, the base 5 equivalent of 894_{10} is 12034_5.

The number system bases that are used most commonly in computer science are binary (2), octal (8), and hexadecimal (16). Number systems with bases that are whole number powers of 2 are convenient to use in computer science because, as explained in the text, computers actually operate in base 2 (binary).

Index

A

Abstraction levels, 39
Accumulator, 26, 35
  defined, 151
Acoustic coupler, 151
A/D. See Analog-to-digital
Addend, defined, 151
Addition, 10-11, 35
  binary, 8
Addressing, 25, 29
  defined, 151
  immediate (direct), 29, 154, 155
  indexed, 29, 155
  page-directed. See Page-directed addressing
Address space, 70
  defined, 151
Admission, discharge and transfer (ADT), 185, 188
ADT. See Admission, discharge and transfer
Algorithm, 39, 41-43, 135-148
  defined, 151
Allergy to drugs, 115, 186
Allergygrp record, 133
Alternative systems analyses, 95-96, 196
ALU. See Arithmetic and logic unit
American Druggist Blue Book Data Center, 97

American National Standards Institute (ANSI), 66
American Society of Hospital Pharmacists, 97
American Standard Code for Information Interchange (ASCII), 17-18, 76, 163-170
  defined, 151
Analog, defined, 151
Analog-to-digital (A/D) interface, 77
  defined, 151
Analysis. See Systems analysis
AND operator, 3, 4
ANSI. See American National Standards Institute
Arabic-decimal number system, 201
Arithmetic/logical operations, 29, 34-36
Arithmetic and logic unit (ALU), 22
  defined, 151
Arithmetic operations. See Mathematics
Arrays, 44, 46, 48, 106
  defined, 151
ASCII. See American Standard Code for Information Interchange
Assemblers, 29, 39-40
  defined, 152
Asynchronous mode, 3-5, 8
Asynchronous serial communication, 85
  defined, 152

Authorize, 138, 146
Automatic reorder system, 186
Availability of software, 70

B

Backup file, 120, 121
Backup system, 99-100
Banked memory, defined, 152
Base (control current input), 5
  defined, 152
BASIC, 46-55
  command syntax in, 47-54
  sample program in, 173-174
  variations of, 54-55
Batch mode, 41
  defined, 152
Baud rate, defined, 152
BCD. *See* Binary coded decimal
BEGIN, 62
Beginners all-purpose symbolic instruction code. *See* BASIC
Benchmark, 70
  defined, 152
Bench testing, 101, 102
Benefits of systems analysis, 184
Bid system, 189
Billing, 186, 189
  information on, 111
Binadd, 137, 147
Binary addition, 8
Binary coded decimal (BCD), 16-17
  defined, 152
Binary mathematics, 10-15, 163-170
  defined, 152
  significance of position in, 10
Binary trees, 106, 107, 110, 146
Bindelete, 137
Bindump, 138
Binsearch, 137
Bits, 15
  defined, 152
Boolean logic, 3, 35
  defined, 152
Boole, George, 3

Bootstrapping, 25
  defined, 152
Branching, 29, 36-37
  conditional, 36
  defined, 152
  stack-oriented, 36
  unconditional, 36, 51
Bubble memory, 74
Budget assistance, 187
Bus
  internal, 155
  system. *See* System bus
Byte, 15, 25
  defined, 152

C

Calculators
  vs. computers, 21
  defined, 152
  function of, 21-22
CALL statement, 55
Cancelorder procedure, 140
Carriage return (RETURN or RTN), 49
"Carry" output, 8
Cartlist, 142
Cartreturn procedure, 142, 144
Cartridge disks, 73
CASE construct, 63, 64, 135
Cathode ray terminals (CRT), 75-76
Central processing unit (CPU), 22, 70
  defined, 152
Changecenter, 145
Changedatabase, 146
CHAR, 64
Character readers, 76
Character recognition. *See* Optical character recognition
Clinical information section of patient information file, 115
Clock, 8, 25
  defined, 153
  speed of, 70
  system, 25, 160

COBOL (Common Business Oriented
    Language), 65-66
Coding systems, 16-18
Collector (input path), 5
    defined, 153
COM. *See* Computer output
    microfiche
Combination drugs, 118
Commands. *See* Statements
Common Business Oriented
    Language. *See* COBOL
Communication
    asynchronous serial, 85, 152
    devices for, 83-85
    parallel, 84, 157
    serial, 84-85, 152, 159, 160
    synchronous, 85, 160
Compiler, 39-40
    defined, 153
Complement
    defined, 153
    tens, 160
    twos, 160
Completion report, 195-197
Compounding, 187, 190
Computer, defined, 153
Computer literacy, defined, 153
Computer output microfiche (COM),
    82
    defined, 153
Conditional branching instructions,
    36
CONST, 62
Constant, 43, 64
    defined, 153
Constraints, 190-191
Construction of microcomputer,
    22-27
Contraindication record, 134
Control current input (base), 5
Controller, defined, 153
Controls, 195
    narcotic, 186-187, 190
    system, 98-99
Core memory
    defined, 153
    ferrite, 72

Cost centers, 119, 122
CPS, 153
CPU. *See* Central processing unit
CRT. *See* Cathode ray terminals
Current, defined, 153

D

D/A. *See* Digital-to-analog
Data
    defined, 43
    name and address, 111
    pointer, 106
    quantitative, 196
Data base management systems
    (DBMS), 98, 99
DATA statement, 49
Data structure, 39, 43-46, 106-135
    defined, 153
    drug information, 125-135
    dynamic, 106
    formulary, 116-118
    inventory, 118-119
    ordering, 124-125
    patient information, 112-114
    serial group, 119-120
    supplier, 123-124
    transaction, 120-123
DB25, defined, 153
DBMS. *See* Data base management
    systems
Decimal mathematics, 10-15
    defined, 153
Decision points, 195
Decrement, defined, 154
Definition of problems, 90, 183-184
Dependability of computer
    equipment, 69
Design
    of master file, 97-98
    proposal to initiate, 196-197
    of systems, 96-98, 100-101
Digital, defined, 154
Digital-to-analog (D/A) converters,
    83
    defined, 154

Digitizers, 77, 160
DIMension statement, 47, 48
Direct (immediate) addressing, 29
   defined, 154, 155
Direct memory access (DMA), 34
   defined, 154
Disk drives, 73
Disks, 73
   cartridge, 73
   defined, 154
   floppy (flexible), 73, 155
   optical, 74
Dividend, defined, 154
Division, 13-15, 35
Divisor, defined, 154
DMA. See Direct memory access
Documentation, 39-40, 41, 42, 46, 47
   defined, 154
DO statement, 56
Dot matrix printers, 79-80
DPIF. See Drug Products
   Information File
Drug allergy
   history of, 115
   laboratory, 186
Drugintx record, 134
Drug Products Information File
   (DPIF), 97
Drugs
   combination, 118
   data structure for information on,
      125-135
   interactions of, 186, 189
   locator record for, 125
   master list of, 186, 189
   nonformulary requests for, 190
   nonstock requests for, 187
   retrieval of information on, 187,
      190
   standing orders for, 114
   utilization reports on, 186, 188
Dumb terminals, 76
Duplex, defined, 154
Dynamic data structures, 106
Dynamic RAM, 71
   defined, 154

E

EBCDIC. See Extended binary coded
   decimal information code
Economic order quantity (EOQ),
   119, 123
Economic reorder point (ERP), 119,
   123
Electrostatic printers, 80
ELSE, 63
Emitters (output path), 5
   defined, 154
Encoder, defined, 154
End block, 43
END statement, 54, 62
ENIAC, 21
EOF, 136, 137
EOQ. See Economic order quantity
EOR (exclusive or), 3, 5, 8
EPROM. See Erasable PROM
Erasable PROM (EPROM), 25, 71,
   72
   defined, 154
ERP. See Economic reorder point
Error block, 42
Errors in syntax, 54
Exclusive or. See EOR
Expandability of computer
   equipment, 69
Extemporaneous compounding, 187,
   190
Extended binary coded decimal
   information code (EBCDIC), 17,
   163-170
   defined, 155

F

FCC. See Federal Communications
   Commission
Federal Communications Commission
   (FCC), 84
Ferrite core memory, 72
Field, defined, 155

File, 40, 46
  backup, 120, 121
  defined, 155
  master, 97-98
  patient information, 115
  patient record, 111
  structures of, 46
  supplier, 117
Fillorder, 141
Firmware, defined, 155
Fixed length record, 45
Flag register (F register), defined, 155
Flexible (floppy) diskette, defined, 73, 155
Floor stock, noncharge, 186, 188-189
Floppy (flexible) disks, 73, 155
Font impact printers, 79
FORDO statement, 63
Formed font impact printers, 79
Forms analysis, 93, 94
Formulary, 186, 189
  data structure of, 116-118
FOR statement, 53
FOR-NEXT statement, 53, 63
FORTRAN, 55-65
F register (flag register), 155
Function, defined, 155
FUNCTION statement, 56, 62-63

G

Generic numbers, 118, 119, 122, 125
Getcart, 143
Getcenter, 145
Getitem, 144
Getname, 138
Getreportname, 147
GOSUB statement, 52, 55
GOTO statement, 51, 55, 62, 63
Graphics tablets, 77
Greater than (GT), 52
Greater than or equals (GTE), 52
Group data structure, 119-120
Group purchasing, 186
GT (greater than), 52
GTE (greater than or equals), 52

H

Hand-shaking signals, defined, 155
Hardware, defined, 155
Hemaction record, 133
Heuristic (life cycle) viewpoint, 90
Hexadecimal numbers, 15-16, 163-170
  defined, 155
History of drug allergy, 115
Hospital pharmacies, 95
Human factors in system design, 100-101

I

IBM. *See* International Business Machines
IF statement, 63
IF-THEN statement, 52, 55
Immediate addressing. *See* Direct addressing
Impact printers, 79-80
Implementation, 101-102
Incompatibility record, 133
Increment, defined, 155
Indexed addressing, 29
  defined, 155
Information
  billing, 111
  clinical, 115
  data structure for, 112-114
  drug, 187, 190
  flow of, 188-190
  patient, 112-114, 115
  retrieval of, 187, 190
  storage devices for, 71-75
Initial bench testing, 102
Initialization, 42, 43, 44, 47, 48, 49
Injection volume, 117
Ink jet printers, 80-81
Input, 48, 49
  control current (base), 5
  voice, 78
INPUT statement, 48, 49
Input devices, 75-78

Input/output (I/O) interface, 26
  defined, 155, 156
Input path (collector), 5, 153
Installed testing, 102
Instructions
  See also specific instructions
  branching. See Branching
  combination of, 37-38
  conditional branching, 36
  direct memory access. See Direct memory access instructions
  microcomputer, 27-38
  million per second. See Million instructions per second
  shift, 35
  unconditional branching, 36, 51
Integers, 44
INTEGER statement, 64
Intelligent terminals, 76
Interactions of drugs, 186, 189
Interdependency analysis of subsystems, 188-190
Interfaces, 195
  analog-to-digital (A/D), 77, 151
  input/output. See Input/output interface
Internal bus, defined, 155
International Business Machines (IBM), 17
Interpreters, 39-40
  defined, 155
Interrupt, defined, 156
Interrupt event counting, 94
Intxsearch, 139
Inventory
  data structure for, 118-119
  and ordering, 185, 188
Invert, defined, 156
I/O. See Input/output
IV labels, 185-186
IVlist, 142
IV system, 188
IV worklist, 185-186

L

LABEL, 62
Labels for IV, 185-186
Laboratory drug allergy, 186
Laboratory report structure, 116
Languages, 55-66
  See also specific languages by name
  assembly, 40
LCD. See Liquid crystal display
LED. See Light emitting diode
Legal status, 117
Less than (LT), 52
Less than or equals (LTE), 52
LET statement, 48, 50, 51
Life cycle (wholistic or heuristic) viewpoint, 90
Light emitting diode (LED), defined, 156
Liquid crystal display (LCD), defined, 156
List of drugs, 186, 189
Literacy in computers, 153
Local hospital pharmacy on-site visits, 95
Logic operations, 3-9
  asynchronous, 3-5
  Boolean, 3, 152
Loops, 55
  REPEAT, 135-136
LT (less than), 52
LTE (less than or equals), 52

M

Magnetic tape, 72-73
Mailorder procedure, 144
Mainframe, 70-71
  defined, 156
Manual backup system, 99
Mark sense, 74-75
Master drug list, 186, 189
Master file design, 97-98

Mathematics, 10-15
  See also Number systems
  binary. *See* Binary mathematics
  decimal. *See* Decimal mathematics
Matrix, 45, 46, 48
  defined, 156
Megahertz, defined, 156
Memory, 25, 29-34
  banked, 152
  bubble, 74
  core. *See* Core memory
  direct access to. *See* Direct memory access
  ferrite core, 72
  random access. *See* Random access memory
  read only. *See* Read only memory
  read/write (R/W). *See* Random access memory
  semiconductor, 71-72
  volatile, 160
Memory-addressing modes, defined, 156
Memory-to-register moves, 29
Microcomputers
  construction of, 22-27
  instructions for, 27-38
Microfiche
  computer output. *See* Computer output microfiche
  defined, 156
Microforms, 82
  defined, 156
Microprogramming, 22
  defined, 156
Million instructions per second (mips), 70
  defined, 156
Minuend, defined, 156
Mips. *See* Million instructions per second
Misspelling record, 132, 133
Mnemonic, defined, 156
Modem, defined, 157
Modes
  See also specific modes
  addressing. *See* Addressing

asynchronous, 8
batch, 152
indexed addressing, 29
memory-addressing, 156
Modularization, 97-98
Modular programming, 39
  defined, 157
Modulator of radio frequency, 158
Monitoring of resources, 187
Monitors (operating systems), 25, 39-40
  defined, 157
Monotony, 101
Multiplication, 12-13, 35
Multiprogramming, 41
  defined, 157
Music, 83

N

Name and address data, 111
Narcotic control, 186-187, 190
National Drug Code, 118
Nesting, defined, 157
Neworder, 138
NEXT statement, 53
NO CHANGE operator, 4, 8
Noncharge floor stock, 186, 188-189
Nonformulary drug requests, 190
Nonstock drug request, 187
No operation statement (NOP), 37
NOP. *See* No operation statement
NOT operator, 3, 4, 8, 64
Number systems, 201-204
  See also Mathematics
  Arabic-decimal, 201
  binary, 10
  defined, 201
  hexadecimal. *See* Hexadecimal numbers
  octal, 15-16

O

Object codes, 29
  defined, 157

Objectives
  identification of, 92-93
  statements of, 196
OCR. *See* Optical character
  recognition
Octal numbers, 15-16
  defined, 157
ONERR statement, 54
On line, 41
  defined, 157
On-site visits of local hospital
  pharmacies, 95
Operating systems. *See* Monitors
Operational system, 195
Operational systems analysis, 93-95
Operations
  arithmetic/logical, 29, 34-36
  asynchronous logic, 3-5
  Boolean. *See* Boolean logic
  branching. *See* Branching
  mathematical, 10-15
  shift, 35
  stack-oriented branching, 36
  wait (WAI), 37
Operators
  AND, 3, 4
  Boolean logic, 3
  defined, 157
  EOR, 3, 5, 8
  NO CHANGE, 4, 8
  NOT, 3, 4, 8, 64
  OR, 3, 4
  unary, 4, 160
Optical character readers, 76
Optical character recognition (OCR), 75
  defined, 157
Optical characters, 74-75
Optical disks, 74
Oralab record, 134
Ordering
  data structure for, 124-125
  and inventory, 185, 188
Orderpoint, 144
OR operator, 3, 4
Output block, 43

Output, "carry," 8
Output devices, 78-83
Output path (emitter), 5

P

Page-directed addressing, 29
  defined, 157
Parallel communication, 84
  defined, 157
Parallel processing, 99
Parallel testing, 101
Parity, defined, 157
Pascal, 56-65, 105
  sample program in, 177-179
Pascal, Blaise, 56
Patient information
  clinical information section of, 115
  data structure for, 112-114
Patient profile, 185, 188
Patient records, 111-116
PC. *See* Program counter
Performance requirements and
  constraints statement, 90
Permanent platter disk drives, 73
PERT. *See* Program evaluation and
  review technique
Pharmacy and Therapeutics (P&T)
  Committee, 116, 118
Platter disk drives, 73
Plotters, 81
  defined, 158
Pointer data type, 106
Pop (pull), defined, 158
Position significance in binary
  number system, 10
Postrecovery testing, 102
Power on jump, 27
  defined, 158
Precedence rules, defined, 158
PRINT statement, 54, 55
Printers, 78-81
Printing terminals, 76
Problem definition, 90, 183-184
Problem list, 116

PROCEDURE, 62, 63
Procedures
  See also specific procedures
  "bin," 146
  cancelorder, 140
  cartreturn, 142, 144
  fillorder, 141
  mailorder, 144
  purchasing, 145
  report generator, 148
  service, 137-138
  transaction, 143, 195
  working, 138-148
Processing, 42, 53
  parallel, 99
  transaction, 195
Profile of patients, 185, 188
Program counter (PC), 26
  defined, 157
Program evaluation and review technique (PERT), 101
Programmable ROM (PROM), 25
  defined, 158
  erasable. See Erasable PROM
Programming
  assembly language, 40
  modular, 39, 157
  structured, 38, 159
  style of, 38-46
Programs (software)
  availability of, 70
  BASIC, 173-174
  batch mode, 41
  benchmark, 70
  defined, 159
  Pascal, 105, 177-179
PROM. See Programmable ROM
Proposal to conduct systems analysis 183-192
Proposal to initiate design, 196-197
Proposal to perform systems analysis, 90-91
P&T Committee. See Pharmacy and Therapeutics Committee
Pull (pop), defined, 158

Purchasing
  group, 186
  procedure for, 145
Push, defined, 158

Q

Qualitative systems analysis, 95
Quantitative data, 196
Quotient, defined, 158

R

Radio frequency modulator (RF modulator), defined, 158
RAM. See Random access memory
Random access memory (RAM), 25, 71
  defined, 158
  dynamic, 71, 154
  static, 71, 159
READ statement, 49
Read only memory (ROM), 25, 71, 72
  defined, 158
  programmable. See Programmable ROM
Read/write (R/W) memory. See Random access memory
REAL, 64
Realtime, 41
  defined, 158
Real variables, 44
RECORD, 64
Records, 45
  allergygrp, 133
  contraindication, 134
  defined, 158
  drugintx, 134
  drug locator, 125
  fixed length, 45
  hemaction, 133
  incompatibility, 133
  misspelling, 132, 133

oralab, 134
patient, 111-116
structures of, 45, 46
terato, 134
variable length, 45
Redundant equipment, 99
Registers, 26
  defined, 159
  flag, 155
  microprogramming, 22
  PC (program counter), 26
  SP (stack pointer), 27
REM (remember) statement, 47
Reorder system, 186
REPEAT statement, 63, 135-136
REPEAT-UNTIL statement, 63
REPEAT-UNTIL EOF statement, 135
Reportfile, 147
Reports
  analysis, 192
  drug utilization, 186, 188
  generator procedure for, 148
  laboratory, 116
  special, 190
  systems analysis completion, 195-197
Requests for drugs
  nonformulary, 190
  nonstock, 187
Resource monitoring, 187
RESTORE satement, 49
Retrieval of drug information, 187, 190
RETURN statement, 52
RF. *See* Radio frequency
ROM. *See* Read only memory
RS232, defined, 159
RTN. *See* Carriage return
Rules, 158
R/W. *See* Random access memory

S

Samples
  BASIC program, 173-174
  Pascal program, 177-179

proposal to conduct systems analysis, 183-192
Scheduling system, 187
Scope of analysis, 191
Semiconductor memory, 71-72
Serial communication, 84-85
  asynchronous, 85, 152
  defined, 159
  synchronous, 160
Serial group data structure, 119-120
Serviceability of computer equipment, 69
Service procedures, 137-138
Sets, 46
Shift operation, 35
Signals
  clock, 8
  hand-shaking, 155
Significance, defined, 159
Software. *See* Programs
SP. *See* Stack pointer
Special reports, 190
Speed of clock, 70
Stack, defined, 159
Stack-oriented branching operations, 36
Stack pointer (SP), 27
  defined, 159
Standing patient drug orders, 114
Statements
  See also specific statements
  CALL, 55
  CASE, 63, 64, 135
  DATA, 49
  DIMension, 47, 48
  DO, 56
  END, 54, 62
  FOR, 53
  FOR-DO, 63
  FOR-NEXT, 53, 63
  FUNCTION, 56, 62-63
  GOSUB, 52
  GOTO, 51, 55, 62, 63
  IF, 63
  IF-THEN, 52, 55
  INPUT, 48, 49

INTEGER, 64
LET, 47, 50, 51
NEXT, 53
no operation, 37
objectives, 196
ONERR, 54
of performance requirements and constraints, 90
PRINT, 54, 55
READ, 49
REM (remember), 47
REPEAT, 63, 135-136
REPEAT-UNTIL, 63
REPEAT-UNTIL EOF, 135
RESTORE, 49
RETURN, 52
syntax of in BASIC, 47-54
THEN, 63
TYPE, 62, 64
WHILE, 140
WHILE-DO, 63
WRITELN, 135
Static RAM, 71
 defined, 159
Stock, 186, 188-189
Storage devices, 71-75
Strength field, 116
String, defined, 159
String variables, 44
Structured programming, 38
 defined, 159
Structures
 data. *See* Data structures
 drug information, 125-135
 file, 46
 formulary, 116-118
 inventory, 118-119
 laboratory report, 116
 ordering, 124-125
 patient information, 112-114
 record, 45, 46
 serial group, 119-120
 supplier, 123-124
 transaction, 120-123
Subroutines, 37, 55

Subsystems, 184-185
 interdependency analysis of, 188-190
Subtraction, 11-12, 35
Subtrahend, defined, 159
Supplierin transaction, 123
Suppliers
 data structure on, 123-124
 file for, 117
 identifier for, 117
Synchronous circuits, 8
 defined, 159
Synchronous communication, 85
 defined, 160
Syntax
 command, 47-54
 defined, 160
 errors in, 54
System bus, 25
 defined, 160
System clock. *See* Clock
System design, 96-98
 human factors in, 100-101
Systems
 backup, 99-100
 control of, 98-99
 defined, 89
 operational, 195
 utilities in, 187, 190
Systems analysis, 39
 alternative, 95-96, 196
 benefits of, 184
 completion report on, 195-197
 defined, 93, 160
 operational, 93-95
 proposal to perform, 90-91
 qualitative, 95
 report on, 192
 sample proposal to conduct, 183-192
 scope of, 191

T

Tape, 72-73
Team formation, 91-92

Tens complement, 160
Terato record, 134
Terminals, 75-76
Testing, 101-102
THEN statements, 63
Time-sharing, 41
　defined, 160
Track, defined, 160
Transaction
　data structure for, 120-123
　procedure for, 143
　processing procedures for, 195
　supplierin, 123
Transactmove, 145
Transdump, 146
Transistors, 5-9
　defined, 160
Truth table, 3, 4, 5, 8
　defined, 160
Twos complement, 160
　TYPE statement, 62, 64

U

Unconditional branching instructions, 36, 51
University of California at San Diego, 65
UNTIL, 136
Utilities, 187, 190

V

VAR, 62
Variable length records, 45
Variables, 44, 64
　defined, 160
　real, 44
　string, 44
Video devices, 81-82
Video digitizers, 77
　defined, 160
Voice, 83
　input of, 78
Volatile memory, defined, 160
Volume of injections, 117

W

WAI. *See* Wait
Wait (WAI) operation, 29, 37
Warnptr, 139
WHILE statement, 140
WHILE-DO statement, 63
Wholistic (life cycle) viewpoint, 90
Wirth, Niklaus, 56
WITH clause, 63
Word size, defined, 160
Working procedures, 138-148
WRITELN statement, 135

X

Xerographic printers, 81

About the Author

JOSEPH A. CORNELL received the Doctor of Pharmacy degree in 1974 from the University of California at San Francisco. He then completed an American Society of Hospital Pharmacists (ASHP)-accredited residency in hospital pharmacy at St. Mary's Hospital in Rochester, Minnesota. Following this, Dr. Cornell joined the faculty of the University of Minnesota, serving a dual role on the staff of the University Hospital Pharmacy Department involving both clinical practice and teaching. After serving briefly on the staff of ASHP, he came to his current position as manager of public computer facilities for the University of Minnesota.

Dr. Cornell's long-standing interest in computer science and systems analysis is illustrated by several of his undergraduate projects and his residency project, an analysis of the information needs of the pharmacy department in a large teaching hospital. Dr. Cornell not only has published research in the field of systems and computer science, but also has created hospital pharmacy computer programs. He decided to write this book in response to the question frequently asked by pharmacists, "How can I learn more about the use of computers in pharmacy?"

Date Due

BRODART, INC.　　　Cat. No. 23 233　　　Printed in U.S.A.